something to live for

RICHARD J. LEIDER
DAVID A. SHAPIRO

something to live for

FINDING YOUR WAY
IN THE SECOND HALF
OF LIFE

BK

Berrett–Koehler Publishers, Inc.
San Francisco
a BK Life book

Berrett-Koehler Publishers, Inc.
235 Montgomery Street, Suite 650
San Francisco, CA 94104-2916
Tel: (415) 288-0260   Fax: (415) 362-2512   www.bkconnection.com

Ordering Information
Quantity sales. Special discounts are available on quantity purchases by corporations, associations, and others. For details, contact the "Special Sales Department" at the Berrett-Koehler address above.
Individual sales. Berrett-Koehler publications are available through most bookstores. They can also be ordered directly from Berrett-Koehler: Tel: (800) 929-2929; Fax: (802) 864-7626; www.bkconnection.com
Orders for college textbook/course adoption use. Please contact Berrett-Koehler: Tel: (800) 929-2929; Fax: (802) 864-7626.
Orders by U.S. trade bookstores and wholesalers. Please contact Ingram Publisher Services, Tel: (800) 509-4887; Fax: (800) 838-1149; E-mail: customer.service@ingrampublisherservices.com; or visit www.ingrampublisherservices.com/Ordering for details about electronic ordering.

Berrett-Koehler and the BK logo are registered trademarks of Berrett-Koehler Publishers, Inc.

Printed in the United States of America

Berrett-Koehler books are printed on long-lasting acid-free paper. When it is available, we choose paper that has been manufactured by environmentally responsible processes. These may include using trees grown in sustainable forests, incorporating recycled paper, minimizing chlorine in bleaching, or recycling the energy produced at the paper mill.

Library of Congress Cataloging-in-Publication Data
Leider, Richard.
    Something to live for : finding your way in the second half of life /
Richard J. Leider, David A. Shapiro.
        p. cm.
    Includes bibliographical references and index.
    ISBN 978-1-57675-456-6 (pbk. : alk. paper)
    1. Older people—Conduct of life.   I. Shapiro, David A., 1957–   II. Title.

BJ1691.L39 2008
646.7'9—dc22
                        2008013065

First Edition
12 11 10 09 08   10 9 8 7 6 5 4 3 2 1

Designed by Detta Penna
Copyedited by Patricia Brewer
Indexed by Joan Dickey

In gratitude to our mothers, fathers,

grandparents, and all wise elders

who led us here.

And to Sally, Andrew, and Greta,

and Jennifer and Mimi,

who show us the way forward.

–RJL

–DAS

contents

foreword by richard bolles

This book, *Something to Live For*, begins a new conversation between its authors and their readers. But Richard Leider and I have talked about this subject for literally decades. All that has changed over the years has been the jargon; the essence has always remained the same: *Something to Live For. A Life with Purpose. Your Mission in Life. Finding Your Vocation.*

I like any work that sets all of this in the context of faith. I am a believer in God, a lover even, and I make no bones about it.

I am also a storyteller. Some of my stories are true. Some of my stories may be true. Here is one such story: I like to think that our souls existed before our bodies. And that, before we came to Earth to inhabit this body, our souls, our breath, our light, stood before the great Creator of the Universe, and volunteered for this Mission. God and we together then decided what that Mission should be, and what particular *gifts* would be needed in order to accomplish that mission. Which God agreed to give us at birth. And so, our Mission was not a command given peremptorily by an unloving Creator to a slave without a vote, but was a task jointly designed by Creator and Creature—us

—in which as fast as our Great Creator said, "I wish," our hearts swelled up with "Oh, yes!"

But when we were born we became amnesiac about anything that transpired before our birth; and therefore amnesiac about the nature of our Mission and our Gifts. Therefore our *search* now for something to live for, for a life with Purpose, for our Vocation, for a Mission in life, is the search for a memory.

God, knowing we would be amnesiac, thoughtfully provided us two gifts, not one. First of all, as I have said, God gave us each an abundance of gifts, including the gifts we needed for our mission. Secondly, God gave us a clue as to the latter, by giving us a special love for those particular gifts. To put it simply, if there is something you love to do, that probably is one of the gifts you need for your Mission. Put them all together, all the gifts you love, and you may see clearly an outline, like all the pieces in a patchwork quilt, of what your Mission is, and what you have to live for.

To change the metaphor, the gifts that God gave you a great love for, are like pearls which you are to string on a necklace. You can arrange them in any order on your necklace, but the most important pearl should lie in the center of the necklace. And, over your lifetime, which one you select to be the most important pearl may change as you change. And so, the necklace changes. Thus, your Mission may not always stay the same *on the surface*; just the same, underneath.

One of the contributions that vocational psychologists—Donald Super, Sidney Fine, John Crites, John L. Holland—have made over the years, is to show us how our vocations may *seem* to change, as we move through life, yet in truth remain the same. In Holland's discoveries, for example, the same three skills are needed for a vocation as psychologist, dental hygienist, clergy, nurse, copywriter, dance therapist, painter, or artist. It all depends on which skill you put in the center of your necklace, which skills you put on either side, etc., etc. That is to say, which skill God gave you the greatest love for, and so forth, on down.

To change the metaphor again, the gifts God gave you for your chosen Mission, the gifts God gave you a great love for, are like a set of building blocks that you can arrange in any way and in any order you choose.

Your uniqueness is found in the way you put your gifts together. You may have the very same gifts as someone else, but each of you will stack them in different ways and that means an entirely different work.

Your life and career changes are just a matter of rearranging the building blocks.

I believe this book you hold in your hands can help you do two things. First, it can help you recall that ancient conversation we have all had with our Creator, enabling you to recall your life's mission and the gifts you've been given to complete it. And second, it can help you rearrange your gifts for the part of that mission you'll be working on in the next phase of your life.

Meanwhile, the conversation that Richard Leider and I began decades ago continues.

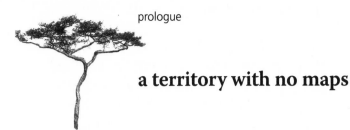

a territory with no maps

The second half of life has become a territory with no maps.

For men and women now moving through midlife and beyond, the path forward is uncharted. It is a journey that has never, in the course of human history, been taken on this scale and with such abandon.

Until the late twentieth century, there was no concept of midlife and beyond because most people died at a relatively young age. In 1900, average life expectancy was around 47 years, about the same as it had been since the dawn of time. Today, the average lifespan in industrialized nations hovers at 80 and above. So, for nearly all of human history, most people died around what we now consider midlife. Adults today are the first full generation of human beings to venture into such a long and vital second half of life.

We are setting forth into *terra incognita* and as a result, many of us feel quite lost.

For the majority of people, the path through the first half of life is somewhat predictable—it's about building a life structure; the second half, though, appears more random. Fewer choices are made for us, but the freedom this gives us is not necessarily liberating.

Some people, to be sure, simply keep doing what they've always done without much reflection. But for many of us, the first-half structure needs to be reinvented. We find ourselves feeling uneasy about what's next. We recognize that the time before us, though perhaps—if we're lucky—rather extended, is indeed limited and this inspires in us a deep need to find our way forward.

Inevitably, the second half of life involves loss—loss of friends and/or family, physical changes and ailments, a growing sense that life may be passing us by—but if we can find the courage to confront and move through those losses, we are apt to discover a new sense of vitality and direction. Exploring the questions that spring up before us can lead to the revelation that we have powerful choices in abundance.

The awareness that we can find a new guidance system for the second half of life is exhilarating. Buried inside the quantitative change in the number of years we live is the possibility of a qualitative one: the evolution of a different perspective on life than the one that brought us to midlife in the first place. For people moving into this new territory, an externally directed guidance system loses its aura in favor of an internally directed one. This new inner-directed capacity to be grounded in one's own sense of self is also linked to a compassion for others.

And so, paradoxically, it is within our relationships with others that we discover our own selves in this previously uncharted territory of life's second half. Through these connections, we make the connections with ourselves required to navigate forward in midlife and beyond.

And that, in short, is what we, as authors, hope to offer to you, as reader, in this book. We hope, simply, to share our experience—and the experience of those whose stories we relate—of finding guidance and direction in the second half of life as a way to assist you in doing the same. We have taken this journey together as friends and co-authors, and the outcome of that journey is this book. Now we invite you to embark upon the journey with us. It is a journey back to the eternal questions: *Where did I come from? Where am I going? What is my purpose for living?*

Back to the essential conversation that reveals the answers in dialogue with ourselves, each other, and wisdom through the ages. Back to the place where the quest was begun—individually, and as a species—where human beings first emerged and embarked on the epic journey that leads to each of us being here, now, pondering these same eternals.

Back then, to Africa, to the ancient rhythm of life, on a journey for those long-sought answers—only this time, at last, together.

In 1994, we published our first work together, *Repacking Your Bags: Lighten Your Load for the Rest of Your Life.* It began with a story Richard told about trekking along the Serengeti plains with a Maasai tribesman named Koyie. Koyie's question about the pack full of high-tech gear that Richard was carrying, "Does all this make you happy?" became a theme for many of the inquiries about lightening one's load that were central to the book's message.

A few years later, we wrote *Whistle While You Work: Heeding Your Life's Calling,* which explored the nature of meaningful work within the context of a life well-lived. Another story from Africa launched the text. This time, Richard told a tale of coming across lions in the Salai plains and having no choice but to press on through the danger. The message that emerged was that "if you can't get out of it, get into it," and this, too, was a recurring theme throughout the book.

In 2001, our third book, *Claiming Your Place at the Fire: Living the Second Half of Your Life on Purpose,* was published. Once more, it began with a story from Africa. This time, Richard related his experience of sitting around the campfire in Tanzania with elders from the Hadzabe tribe of hunter-gatherers. The message of the tale was that becoming an elder is a matter of claiming one's place in the social system through the sharing of wisdom and narrative. And again, lessons learned in Africa were central to the text; we drew deeply upon Richard's experiences with African elders to help illuminate our own perspective on vital aging and the second half of life.

So, with all this talk about and focus upon Africa, and given that we have had a deep personal and professional relationship stretching back more than two decades now, you might think that the two of us have probably spent a good deal of time together in that large and mysterious continent.

The truth is, however, until this past year, we had never been in Africa together. Dave's connection to the African lands and people had been totally vicarious, through Richard. While this hadn't prevented us from writing the stories and using them to help us convey our messages, there's no doubt that it did affect our ability to relate the experiences together.

But at last, that has changed. We have finally gotten back to the rhythm together.

In the Spring of 2006, we had the opportunity, along with a dozen other men, aged around 50 and above, from the USA, Canada, and Europe, to travel together in northern Tanzania and to experience together the authentic source experience that Africa offers. And from this, in no small part, has emerged this book, *Something to Live For: Finding Your Way in the Second Half of Life.*

Admittedly, this is an experience we were privileged as Westerners to have had and one we are deeply grateful for having been able to share. And certainly it is one informed by the fact that we are both men and that our safari, though not by design a "men's journey," was one undertaken by and with a group of men. And while we must admit that our narrative springs from a certain perspective we have as men together with men, we do sincerely believe that questions we had and the answers we found have application across cultures and gender.

In the pages that follow, we explore a number of themes and lessons that have come out of our time spent with several African tribes. We hope they shed light on our ongoing learning about why it is essential to have something to live for.

We also hope that from our long-awaited shared experience will emerge two additional themes that, for us, marked what it meant to be in Africa together. We call these *authenticity* and *wholeheartedness* and see them, in many ways, as defining not only what being together in Africa was like, but also as linking together much of what lies at the foundation of our message in this book.

For Dave, finally getting to Africa meant that he no longer had to just imagine what it was like. He no longer had to apologize and explain to people why it was he'd never been and how it was he thought he could still write about it honestly. Being in Africa enabled him to fully inhabit a story that had always been merely told to him; it removed sensory blinders and brought forth the full bouquet of sights, sounds, smells, and tastes he had enjoyed only virtually. Above all, this made for a truly authentic experience and allowed Dave to become more authentic himself in thinking and writing about it.

For Richard, the theme of wholeheartedness marked our shared experience in Africa. Being there together gave him the freedom to fully reveal his deep and abiding love for the land and people we encountered. Instead of merely relating stories to Dave, he was able to include his writing partner in them. Instead of having to occasionally temper his enthusiasm, he was able to really open his heart and let the joy he so often experiences in Africa pour forth, sharing his feelings without having to explain them or put them in context. In this way, he was able to put his whole self into the experience, embracing it wholeheartedly.

Being in Africa together also represented a step forward in our personal and professional relationship. It meant that we had the time to get to know each other better and to talk about our lives and our

passions in deeper, more authentic and wholehearted ways. It also
meant we had more opportunities than ever before to discuss the core
of our work together. From those opportunities has emerged this book,
Something to Live For: Finding Your Way in the Second Half of Life.

And for you, the reader, we hope this means we are able to offer
you a work that engages you even more fully than any of our previous
books. To the extent that *Something to Live For* flows out of our own
life quests, we hope that it may connect with you in deeper, more profound ways. To the extent that we are discovering new ways to be more
authentic and wholehearted, we offer to you a work we have tried to
make more authentic and wholehearted, as well.

And so, we welcome you on a journey back to the rhythm, to a
place where self-discovery is made possible through experience and
reflection. The intent of this expedition is to help provide insight into
eternal questions we all face at times in our lives, but never more pro-
vocatively than in the second half.

We explore these questions in three main parts. In *Part 1: Savoring the World*, you are invited to return to a time and place where our
connections to the natural world and its patterns of time and space are
revealed more clearly to us and where we are better able to clarify for
ourselves what really matters in our lives.

In *Part 2: Saving the World*, we take on our generosity to fellow
travelers and what it means to shape a life that makes a positive difference to the lives of others. Drawing upon the ways and practices of
both traditional and contemporary societies, we seek to bring forth the
time-honored lessons of tribes and elders who have sustained themselves for centuries.

In *Part 3: Finding Your Way*, we examine what it really means and
takes to be truly fulfilled in the second half of our lives. We offer up
practices that can help us live a life of purpose and meaning—saving
the world—while simultaneously infusing our experiences with vitality

and joy—savoring it. There are many pathways to finding our way in life, especially during the second half, and in this part of the book, we explore such routes to vital aging.

Ultimately, the path we share in this book may seem both familiar and unfamiliar—as it has to us along the way. It is our hope that in traveling together, we arrive at a destination we have been long seeking, one that enables us, wholeheartedly and authentically, to discover something to live for.

part 1

savoring the world

Little by little, wean yourself.
   This is the gist of what I have to say.
   From an embryo, whose nourishment comes in the
blood,
      move to an infant drinking milk,
      to a child on solid food,
            to a searcher after wisdom,
                  to a hunter of more invisible game.

Rumi

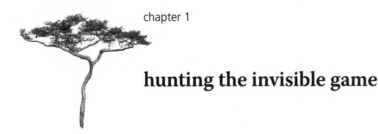

hunting the invisible game

Who Do I Want to Be Now that I'm Grown Up?

How are we to see life? Is it an existence of meaningless movement from one moment to the next? Or is there a larger purpose in life, something to live for?

When we're young, we think that when we're all grown up, we'll have all the answers. We'll know what we want to do, how we want to do it, and with whom we want to do it.

But when we're older, we realize it doesn't work that way. The questions don't go away, and the answers don't magically appear. Just because we're grown up doesn't mean we're finished growing.

Throughout our lives, we continue to ask these eternal questions: "Why am I here?" "What is my purpose?" "What am I living for?" And while we make these inquiries on and off from cradle to grave, they somehow become more pressing, more urgent, and certainly more poignant in the second half of our lives.

In the first half of life, the questions are framed by basic economic realities. Eventually, though, we reach a point—usually around midlife—where the answers are no longer obvious. Somewhat freed from the practical (although usually not the *emotional*) responsibilities of providing for our basic needs, we find ourselves having to come up with our *own* answers.

We reach a point in our lives when we might phrase the question like this: *Who do I want to be now that I'm grown up?*

Consequently, we struggle, living in the gap between who we are and what we do. Some of us experience daily life as energy-draining and spirit-crushing. Some remain in service to the story of the first half of our lives, when our souls have already moved on to the story of the second half. And so, the hunger for answers to the "Who do I want to be?" question grows stronger.

But where do the answers come from?

Modern media being what it is, especially in light of the mass of Baby Boomers entering this second half of life, potential responses abound. Advice about life is now so cheap and abundant, it floods us from email greetings, tea bags, coffee cups, and the sides of city buses: "Pursue goodness, and you will achieve great things." "Achieving true success is being yourself." "You can only be as happy as the least happy person in the house, and two bathrooms are mandatory."

Few such aphorisms are worthless and many offer genuine insight. Yet, with so much coming at us, even the most profound wisdom rarely finds its way in. We filter our world by merely skimming the surface, reading capsule summaries. We might encounter the answers we are looking for if only we could step back and revisit the timeless rhythm of life.

In short, we might find our answers by revisiting the wisdom of our ancestors, specifically the hunters and gatherers that we are and always have been. What's especially tricky, of course, is that what we're seeking is far more elusive than what we, and traditional hunter-gathering people like the Hadzabe in Tanzania, have traditionally sought. It's straightforward (though by no means simple) to hunt animals and gather foodstuffs. The search for the subtle something we are seeking is, as the Rumi poem suggests, at a level far beyond mere sustenance, or even wisdom.

What we are hunting is "the invisible game." And we might think of this in both senses of the word "game": we are hunting for an elusive creature, one that is difficult to even see, much less capture; but we are also hunting for an intangible game of sorts—the meaningful life game.

In our own hunt for the "invisible game," we read extensively in psychology, philosophy, and ancient spiritual traditions. We interviewed over a hundred people from all walks of life, focusing on the question, "What do you live for?" And we traveled to Tanzania, East Africa, to learn from elders in traditional communities, notably to find out what the remaining hunter-gatherer peoples had to teach us about hunting the invisible game. We wanted to write about the simple, yet profound truths that would fit together, build upon each other, and tell a story about how human beings can find their way in the second half of life.

Our trip to Africa was an Inventure Expedition, a combination of outward exploration—adventure—and inward reflection—inventure. Our intention was to experience our own midlife odyssey. We wanted to deepen our conversation around the question, "Why do some people find something to live for in the second half, while others do not?" This was the invisible game we were hunting, and we learned to pursue the answers with the tenacity of the literal hunters with whom we were living.

And not surprisingly, some of the most profound experiences we had, and the answers they led us to, were not what we thought we were looking for at all.

How Do I Get Down?

On our pathway through life, some of the ways we take are superhighways, clogged with fellow travelers; others are roads less traveled. At times the way forward is quite clear; at other times, we are forced to navigate through uncharted territory.

Sometimes we're on a path but don't know it; other times, we may think we're on a path but aren't; sometimes we make the path as we go along; and then there are those times when we're just plain lost.

Whatever the particulars, though, there does come a time—probably many times—in all of our lives, when we have to find our own path. We have to survey uncharted territory and figure out how to get where we want to go, even if we're not entirely sure where that is.

This is the case as we grow older. The way from youth to midlife is pretty clear; the path forward from there is not so obvious. When we're younger, we see the arc of our lives as an ascent. We "climb the ladder of success" in our careers; we rise "from the outhouse to the penthouse;" if we're lucky and work hard, we'll ascend "to the top of the heap."

At midlife, though, our next pathway may be somewhat murky. After all, if you've made it as high as you're going to get, the only way forward is down—and that may not appear to be an attractive option. Moreover, and more to the point, while descent is inevitable, the safe and rewarding route down can be very hard to find. When you're climbing, the destination is easy to see; you just look up and put one foot in front of the other. You can see where you're going; there are usually plenty of others headed in the same direction, and you have models of people who've already made it to be emulated.

On the way back down, though, it's not the same. The eventual destination can be very difficult to see. When you look below, the path tends to be obscured. What was obvious on the way up isn't so clear on the way down. Moreover, descending, you're pretty much on your own. Each of us has to find his or her own way. And because of this, it's much harder to get the kind of support that enabled us to ascend so easily in the first place.

Perhaps not surprisingly, this metaphorical journey is often illustrated in real life. Many of us have had a hiking experience similar to this one Dave describes.

✳❈✦ We've arrived, after a long day's drive, at our campground above the Serengeti, a high plateau overlooking vast grasslands of every conceivable shade of green and gold. It's an amazing place that our guide and trip leader, David (Daudi) Peterson, refers to as "God's sculpture garden." Massive rock formations rise up from the savannah, which rolls into the vast distance, as far as the eye can see. The rocks remind me of giant ships, sailing through the endless acacia trees which dot the landscape.

We are 14 men from the industrialized West who have come to learn from wise elders in Tanzania, Africa. Ranging in age from about 50 to around 70, we all hold positions of some success and mastery in our communities and are, in general, respected for our accomplishments and competence in life. And yet, as we each move further into the second half of our lives, we have begun to re-examine the roles we play in society, and the roles which, as new elders, our societies permit us to play. So, we have come to Africa in hopes of meeting with the leaders of indigenous groups whose social organization provides a clearer role for those who have gained the experience and wisdom that come with age.

We have been traveling together for about a week and have learned much about one another and ourselves. Each of us has had a taste of what Africa can offer in terms of adventure and "inventure," and we are all, to varying degrees, amazed and humbled by what we have seen.

I for one, though, am still looking for that life-changing experience which has so far eluded me. Richard has told me stories of his many safaris in Africa and I've marveled at the authentic adventures he's had: backpacking across the Ngorongoro Crater without support, being surrounded by lions, confronting elephant poachers in the middle of nowhere. Our trip has been incredible, no doubt about it, but I've found it, after a week, just a bit tame. If I'm going to truly experience the wildness of Africa, the time is nigh.

Everyone has stowed his gear and begun poking around the campsite. Some are drinking beer and watching the nascent illuminations of what promises to be another awe-inspiring African sunset. Others are wandering about checking out the native flora and fauna. A few have taken a hike up a well-worn path to the top of a 200-foot-high rock that dominates the north side of our campsite. The top of this rock, whose vantage point has earned it the nickname of our "balcony," commands a 360-degree view of the area; the only spot higher than it is another rock to the east of our campsite, one without such a clear path to the top.

Wanting some physical activity after our long day in the Land Rovers, and feeling at last that this is the time for some real African adventure, I decide to try to find a way to the top of the east rock. I begin to wind my way around and through thorny bushes and up and over rock outcroppings as I ascend. As I climb, I can pretty well see where I want to get to; although the summit of the rock is sometimes obscured by overhanging branches, it ultimately reappears as I scrabble through the underbrush. Eventually, after about 20 minutes, I come around a final corner of stone and reach the top of the rock.

The view is incredible, even better than the one from the balcony. Not only does it afford me the same vast perspective in all directions, it also gives me a dominating view of our entire campsite. I take pleasure in watching my fellow "inventurers" move about the camp below me. I flatter myself by imagining myself to be the intrepid explorer who, alone among us all, was able to ascend to this lofty perch. Sure, I think, I could have taken the well-worn route up to the balcony, but that would have been too easy for a true explorer like me. I raise my arms to the sky, "Rocky" style, celebrating my accomplishment, reveling in the unique adventure I alone among my fellow travelers have achieved.

After about 15 minutes of self-congratulation, I decide it's about time to return to camp. The sun is beginning to set and we have a fireside chat scheduled at dusk. Since, I figure, it took me 20 minutes or so to ascend, I should be able to be back around the campfire in no more than a quarter hour or so.

I begin to head down, but nothing looks familiar. I can't for the life of me tell where, though the underbrush, I must have emerged as I ascended. I try a couple different routes, but all are either blocked or lead to sheer rock faces with no handholds whatsoever.

There is no clear pathway down; as far as I can see, there is no pathway down at all. I begin to feel my heart beat faster and a bit of panic starting to set in. "How did I get up here?" I ask myself over and over. "Is it even possible to get down? What if no one has ever really climbed this rock? What if that's because it's impossible to get back down?"

Far more than 15 minutes have already passed and it's starting to get darker. The sun is setting and shadows are lengthening ominously. I have visions of having to call down to my fellow travelers—who I'm not even sure could hear me—for help. So much for being the intrepid explorer; instead, I'm going to be the lame-brained loser who has to be saved by the search party.

I begin to feel completely lost. This is adventure, all right, but not what I have planned for. I was supposed to emerge triumphantly back down from the summit, tracing easily the route that got me there. Instead, I see no way forward and at this point, unfortunately, no way back either.

In a way though, being stuck like this turns out to be quite useful. I'm forced to sit quietly for a few moments collecting myself, simply observing all that is around me. My focus shifts from where I want to be to where I actually am. Instead of gazing into the distance at my longed-for destination (which, at this point, I can't see anyway), I have no choice but to turn my attention to where I am and see what emerges from that.

As a result, I manage to locate, just to my left, a slim passageway under some thorn bushes that seems accessible. This can't be the same way I came up, though. There is no easy line that brings me around the stickers; rather, I'm forced to push my way through, embedding my shirt with tiny needles that pierce me all over my chest and back.

I have to move slowly, continually unhooking my clothes from thorns that snag me and impede my progress. On at least one occasion, getting hooked isn't such a bad thing; it slows me from careening through the brush to a slippery rock face that heads straight over a 50-foot cliff.

At one point, I'm essentially flat on my back, inching my feet in front of me as I slide beneath low-lying branches, and then, I find myself sliding on my palms for the last 50 yards or so of the descent, at last emerging from the underbrush with a hard thud against a boulder that sends shivers all the way up my spine.

Sweaty, dirty, bleeding from dozens of small thorn cuts, and shaking from the ordeal, I make my way to my tent and do my best to compose myself before heading off to join my mates around the campfire.

Thankfully, I'm not too late and the dying light hides the evidence on my face and body of my misadventure. Or maybe everyone is just too nice to ask why I seem so shaken.

Later, after a beer, I do tell my friends about my ordeal. Everyone is understanding, if not entirely sympathetic, but we share the observation that my experience is not at all unique. A few others among us have had similar experiences while hiking but all of us recognize what happened to me as analogous to the larger journey through life. On the first half of our life's journey, the destination is clear; we navigate toward it by keeping our eyes on the prize.

In the second half of life, however, our destination is far more mysterious and hidden. It is indeed the "invisible game." And we need a whole different sort of navigation system to find our way, one that helps us introspect, locate where we are, and make our way safely ahead.

By midlife, hardly anyone is unfamiliar with the phenomenon of finding the ascending path easier to navigate than the descending route. To a person, everyone knows what it's like to feel somewhat (or quite a bit) lost on the way down from the highest of heights. It's a common feeling among us to wonder whether we will be able to make it back safely from a destination we achieved with more or less ease. We all know that everything that goes up must eventually come down, but we share a sense of puzzlement over how exactly each of us will navigate that confusing and sometimes troubled path back down.

One of our goals in this book is to explore that descending path. What can we do to make the downward arc of our life's time and energy as rewarding and exciting as things were on the way up? How can we learn to recognize the signs and indicators that show us the way ahead?

Descending is not capitulation; it is as essential to the overall journey as ascending. Both are natural to growing whole, not old. Going up is paradigmatically a matter of savoring the world; going down—and helping others to do so—is more about saving. Learning to both save and savor the world requires a spiritual maturity that involves having scaled and come down from a sufficient number of summits to recognize that a self-absorbed life is not very fulfilling. It takes a spirit of generativity—a willingness to give back cross-generationally—to savor the way down.

In life's second half, we need to learn to look at things in a new way. Instead of fixing our eyes ahead on the summit, we must learn to be more observant of the previously unseen passageways that lead us to newly defined summits. We need to notice more carefully what is inside us that points the way, rather than looking outside of ourselves for the destination. We need a new guidance system for the second half of life.

A New Guidance System for the Second Half of Life

Learning to descend involves a whole set of new skills that requires a whole new perspective. It begins with a new mindset, one that values the present moment as highly as the eventual destination. Instead of constantly striving for our goal, we need to learn to consistently appreciate all we have in the moment. On our Africa adventure, we tried to travel without watches, to remind us of this. When someone asked,

"What time is it?" the answer was always, "Now!" And when someone asked, "Where are we?" the answer was always a resounding, "Here!"

In this way, we are never lost; we are always exactly where we need to be—exactly where we are—and always at the right time—now.

This is the authentic and wholehearted experience of adventure that is accessible to us no matter where we are—in Africa or our living room—at all times through our lives. It is the spirit captured in T. S. Eliot's famous admonition that "old men ought to be explorers."

Fortunately, that spirit is within us all. Indeed, one might argue that it is encoded into the deepest parts of our being from time immemorial.

Something to live for can be found only by understanding the kind of creatures that humans are: contradictory and complicated, in harmony and constant opposition with ourselves, divided in many ways. We are shaped by individual selection to be selfish creatures who compete for resources—pleasure and savoring the world. And we are shaped by group selection to be tribal creatures who long to lose ourselves in something larger—to save the world.

And so, there cannot be a single answer to the question, "What am I living for?" There must be, in fact, two. This more comprehensive answer to life's meaning is alluded to in E. B. White's powerful words:

> If the world were merely seductive, that would be easy.
> If it were merely challenging, that would be no problem.
> But I arise in the morning, torn between a desire to save
>   the world and a desire to savor the world.
> That makes it hard to plan the day.

Happiness comes from within (saving) and from without (savoring). We need the guidance of both to discover something worth living for.

And so, with all due respect to the esteemed Mr. White, we believe that the desire to both save and savor the world makes it *easy* to plan the day. When we realize that in order to be truly fulfilled we must do both, our choices for daily living begin to unfold naturally. From vital elders who show us the great joy one experiences through generosity to one's community, we see that it is by saving the world—committing to a cause larger than ourselves—that we savor it—find the everyday joy that having something to live for gives us.

It comes down to a simple truth: individual fulfillment through a way of life that sustains one's community—in short, savoring and saving the world.

And yet, as simple and obvious as this is, it's easy to miss. Many of us do; others grasp it ephemerally; all of us seem to have an inkling within us, but it slips away; we get it back; it slips away again.

Popular culture reminds us of this story again and again in books, television, and movies. In the film *About Schmidt,* Jack Nicholson plays a reasonably successful businessman who loses all sense of meaning and purpose in his life when the roles and people who had supported his sense of self are removed. He retires due to age; his wife dies; his daughter moves away, marries, and begins her separate life; and he is left an empty shell of a person. He sleepwalks through the day, unable to find anything he cares about or considers worth doing.

At the end of the movie, Schmidt realizes that his only meaning-ful connection is a very tenuous one to an orphan he supports in a Save the Children-like program in Africa. He writes to the child, in a heart-felt and authentic way, and in doing so, seems to connect with a part of himself he was missing. When the child writes back, and Schmidt reads the letter, he weeps as the questions he has avoided come flooding in all at once: Did he ever really live? Did he love? Was he loved? Will he ever really discover something to live for?

Through films like *Schmidt,* and in countless other works of art that raise similar issues, the eternal question of life's meaning is surfaced and resurfaced. Our old sense of self is held up to the mirror and a new one waits to be revealed. Such moments are typically confusing, even painful, but they constitute an invitation to hunt the invisible game—to reorient our purpose and priorities. These moments invite us to ask, "How can I *both* savor and save the world?"

And so, the "invisible game" we are hunting is, in many ways, a hunt for ourselves. In tracking down what we are looking for within us, we find what we are seeking in the world. We gain a true sense of something to live for when our lives align with both saving and savoring the world. Meaning emerges moment-to-moment from this alignment, and so, we can get on with the business of living, even surprised we are still here.

🐾 *Letters to Live For*

In our first book, *Repacking Your Bags,* we included a series of what we called Postcard Exercises. In these, readers were invited to open a dialogue with a partner through the simple act of sending a postcard to that person.

As simple as these postcards were, they proved to be remarkably effective. We heard from many readers who used the postcards to begin and carry on discussions that were important and useful in many ways.

In this book, and in our own practice, we take this concept one step further, and encourage the writing of letters—*Letters to Live For*—with the hope they can help clarify that elusive something to live for we are hunting.

We have found that there is something quite profound about the lost art of letter-writing, something that encourages us to speak wholeheartedly and enables us to see ourselves authentically as we present ourselves in writing to others.

Like Schmidt, who finally discovered his innermost needs and desires by corresponding with the orphan boy in Africa, we reveal ourselves to ourselves in the act of letter-writing and come to discover aspects of ourselves that were lost or forgotten.

When Dave turned 50 this year, he set for himself the task of writing one letter a week to 50 people in his life who had influenced and/or touched him deeply in some way. He set out to communicate, as authentically and wholeheartedly as he could, what each person had meant to him and how grateful he was to have known him or her.

Sorry to say, he didn't fully complete the task, but he did manage about two dozen missives to old (and new) friends, former lovers, and individuals like his wife, daughter, and his co-author and mentor, Richard. They weren't handwritten, but they were printed out on paper and sent through the mail. Somewhat amazingly, in almost every case, he received back—sometimes relatively quickly, sometimes months later—a letter in reply. And in all those cases, his correspondents said how touched they were to hear from him, especially in a real old-fashioned paper and sent-with-a-stamp letter.

So, we encourage you to try something like this, too. Write and send a letter to someone in your life who has touched you in some way. Let them know how you feel about their influence on you and what knowing them has meant to you.

For the theme of this first letter, you might, like Schmidt, pick a young person with whom you feel a connection that is wholehearted and authentic.

We encourage you to write to someone younger than you—your child, grandchild, a student—with heartfelt words about the years they are living. Try to come from your own experience rather than being prescriptive. Use this as an opportunity for self-discovery rather than solemn advice.

Here is a sample from us, from Dave to his daughter, Mimi, who at the time, had just turned 10.

Dear Mimi,

Congratulations on your tenth birthday. You will now be a double-digit age for the rest of the time I know you.

Ten was quite a year for me. It was the year I first danced with a member of the opposite sex—Pam Mayer, in the basement of Sally Perkins's house. The song, if I recall correctly, was "Paperback Writer" by the Beatles. I wonder if that had any bearing on my own career as a writer myself.

The ten years between now and when you turn 20 will, if they are anything like mine, be the most intense ten years you will experience in your whole life. These will be the years in which you really begin to discover your own voice, and use it.

This decade was the decade of deep and abiding friendships. I remember thinking that my real family during this time was my gang of buddies; I'm sure I was influenced more at 15 by the attitudes and opinions of my friends than I was by those of my parents. I was lucky, I think, that most of my pals had their heads screwed on pretty straight—not that we were total nerds or goody-two-shoes, but it's good that we all basically wanted to make some sort on ongoing contributions to the world; this kept most of us from being too self-centered and as selfish as we might have been.

The time you're living through is also the time when I first fell in love—or at least what felt like love at the time. Again, I was pretty lucky here. My first real girlfriend was a kind and caring person who really did like me a lot. I trust you will find real affection in your first romantic relationships, too.

As I said earlier, I was lucky that my parents put up with me all through the years from 10 to 20; I wasn't always the easiest person to tolerate. But even in my worst moments,

I never doubted that they loved me and this enabled me to carry on, in spite of myself sometimes.

I just want to say to you that you need never worry about the depth and solidity of my—and your mother's— love for you. It's probably pretty likely we will have some difficult times over the next decade, some disagreements and arguments. But if you always know that we both love you with all our hearts—even when we don't love what you're doing—I think we'll all be okay.

Mostly, I can't wait to see what the coming years bring. I support you wholeheartedly as you begin to undertake your own ongoing hunt for what has been called "the invisible game." It's going to be a wild ride and taking it with you will be a quite a trip, I'm sure.

Love always,

Dad

See if this *Letter to Live For* is one that works for you. Try writing to a child—your own, one with whom you have a close relationship, or even one you merely know of, through association or perhaps, fiction. What matters is that you put your whole self into the writing and see what you can discover about yourself in the process. If possible, you may want to share the letter with that child; the ensuing conversation may be even more powerful than the letter itself.

chapter 2

how to die happy

Believe that each new day that dawns will be the last for you: Then each unexpected hour shall come to you as a delightful gift.

Horace

Better Than Good

✴)K⸰ Our group of 14 has risen at dawn in the Nou Forest, our tents scattered through a thickly wooded campsite 7500 feet high in the hills above the Rift Valley in northern Tanzania. We have taken a long and invigorating hike through the forest and have spied numerous exotic birds and animals and have even, for a while, tracked an elephant through the surrounding hills and valleys. We have been guided by a trio of men from the local Iraqw tribe, an agrarian people whose tidy farms, nestled on the steep hillsides all around us, we have admired yesterday on our journey here. These men, in their thirties and forties, while not yet official elders in their communities, have begun to assume greater authority among their people. Certainly, the competence and confidence with which they guide us speaks volumes about their readiness to take on full leadership roles.

It is evening now, and, having eaten, we are sitting around a cheerful campfire under a sky blazing with stars. The waning moon has begun to rise in the east; it is just past full and brightens the horizon as it ascends. We are engaged in what we call an "inventure session"—an opportunity to journey inward together as we have journeyed outward together on our safari. Our discussion has been inspired by a lovely poem by Derek Walcott called "Love After Love," in which Walcott admonishes the reader to "Peel your own image from the mirror / Sit. Feast on your life." We are exploring in conversation what this means and how each of us can take a long hard look at the man in the mirror to more fully celebrate the gift of life we have been given.

As we move deeper into our discussion, a common question emerges—one we have broached already and which we will continue to expand upon in the coming three weeks of our safari. It revolves around what it means to be an elder in our own Western society and how this compares to the roles and responsibilities of elders in more traditional societies, like that of the Iraqw with whom we are visiting. Not surprisingly, most of us express some confusion, consternation, and even sadness over the generally devalued way in which people "of a certain age" are perceived in the contemporary world. Richard articulates this view well when he refers to the standard literature about aging, which typically sees life completely in terms of ascent to around middle age, and then descent in one's later years. While none of us is unaware of the inevitable physical changes that eventually slow us all down, we also, to a man, chafe somewhat at the notion that the best years of our lives are past.

At the same time, however, we are products of our society. Each of us, in spite of being vital and engaged older men, cannot help but feel some trepidation and discomfort about what the coming years hold for us. We would all be lying to ourselves and each other if we said that we wholeheartedly, and without hesitation, embraced all that it meant to be an older person in today's modern world.

As a way of addressing our question, we have engaged in dialogue with our three Iraqw hosts. With the help of translation by our safari guide, Daudi Peterson, we have begun to talk about the leadership role that elders play in Iraqw social and political organization. Essentially, all the important decisions in their group are made through what we might call elder councils. Among the Iraqw, those who have lived the longest and seen the most are revered for their wisdom and are consulted on all matters that matter most to the community: land rights and ownership, discipline and punishment, group organization and direction. While these elder councils do not operate in isolation, but draw upon the input and participation of any and all affected by their decisions, they do, however, have the ultimate say about things and their decisions and decision-making processes are deeply respected and revered.

Through Daudi, we ask one of the Iraqw, a proud and handsome man of 48 (although he looks no older than 35 at most) named Karoli, how one becomes an elder among his people. His answer makes us all laugh. Essentially, he says, one becomes an elder by living long enough.

The elders in his community are those who have lived the most years. It is not exactly that one automatically becomes an elder by getting old; however, it is the case that unless one has a certain number of years under his belt, one cannot truly ascend to elderhood. Karoli tells us that, at 48, he is on the cusp of becoming an elder. He has a wife and a family, owns land and livestock, and participates to a significant degree in community decision making. But he is not yet, by virtue of not being quite old enough, an elder among his people.

With our doubts and concerns about being among the old ones in our society in mind, we ask him if he looks forward to becoming an Iraqw elder. Karoli, who up until now has affected a rather serious countenance, smiles broadly but doesn't speak. Daudi clarifies our question, asking in Swahili, "How do you feel about becoming an elder?" Karoli smiles even more. "Safi. Safi sana. Afadhali sana." "Good. Very good. Better than good."

"Better than good."

This expression becomes a sort of mantra for us on our trip. Whenever we need to describe another of the amazing cultural, ecological, and/or spiritual experiences we are having individually and collectively on our safari, the words, "better than good" spring to our lips. We delight inwardly and outwardly at the language Karoli has given us for describing the wonder and glory of the African landscape and experience we are savoring together.

But more poignantly, his words give us a framework for comparison about finding our own voices as elders in Western society. How many of us see the prospect of our later years of one as "better than good"?

This becomes one of the central inquiries in our "inventure sessions" on the remainder of our time together in Africa. In the two and a half weeks ahead of us, we continually come back to the question of what it means to find our elder voices in the West and how, if possible, it can be an experience that is, for all of us, "better than good."

This same question then, has become one of the central puzzles in the pages that follow. How do we, as those with the most years of experience in our own lives and the lives of our communities, find a voice for ourselves that is wholehearted, authentic, and purposeful? How do we draw upon the wisdom of experience to make contributions to society that enrich our lives together? How, ultimately, do we make the years to come the best years of our lives, how do we make them for ourselves and others, indeed "better than good"?

The answer, we believe, is to be found in a life of what psychologist Erik Erikson called "generativity," a life of meaningful connections to and caring for future generations.

Becoming Generative

How many truly happy people do you know? If you can tick off your answers on only one hand, consider a second question: Why are so few people truly happy?

One reason is lack of purpose. Purpose is essential to deep joy. When we lose our reason to get up in the morning, we start dying. Much of today's dissatisfaction stems from failing to discover new ways to both save and savor the world. When purpose dies, vitality dies. And even if no one else notices the deadness in our souls, we notice.

Most of us have a keen awareness of purpose when it is present in others and ourselves, and we have an uneasy feeling of "inner kill"—deadness—when it is absent.

Living on purpose means both saving and savoring the world. Both are essential to vitality. Do you have a reason to get up in the morning? Do you, while savoring your life, have a reason larger than yourself for living? Purpose has many meanings, but one is the essential link between *saving* and *savoring*.

Purpose is the driving force behind the motive to get up in the morning. The ultimate test for happiness is this: "Can you look at your life and feel peace of mind in that you are living a purposeful life?" Can you regard your present state, no matter how limited by financial means or health, as one of living on purpose?

Purpose is what concerns us the most; what we care about; what gets us moving. Purpose is the anchor that secures us to life, which anchors us during crisis, that keeps us going when nothing else does. It fits things together. It gives meaning in times of uncertainty or loss.

Before the days of books, computers, and the Internet, *wisdom*— where the best hunting was, what berries and plants were good to eat, when it was time to move camp and when not—was held by elders, those who had lived long enough to experience and impart an understanding of the essentials. The job of the elder was to teach the essentials and to bring forth the successes of the younger generation. This was the elders' purpose.

Today, the common store of information and knowledge is more complex and more accessible. No longer is information and knowledge the exclusive purview of elders. The accessibility of information and knowledge through the Internet is now much more the domain of the young, the masters of the new cybernetic world. Indeed, the last half century has seen a revolution in the acquisition and transmission of information and knowledge.

Wisdom, however, is another matter. Wisdom's domain lies in another direction. Wisdom is not exclusively about information and knowledge, but about *context*, and in this arena the young must often still defer to the old. Why? Because when it comes to the essentials of living, it is clear we haven't made as much progress since ancient times. Wisdom moves slowly because it takes a lifetime to acquire and there are no shortcuts. In fact, it is the paradox of wisdom, that the faster we try to master it, the slower it comes to us; the very act of accelerated living inhibits the intuitive quality of *ripening* our wisdom.

Wisdom mostly remains the domain of the elders among us, and the technology revolution has not diminished our need for them; it has accelerated it. It has created a need for wise elder voices in the world.

In an article in *Newsweek* magazine, evangelist Billy Graham remarked, "All my life I've been taught how to die, but no one ever taught me how to grow old." What a remarkable insight from a wise elder and mentor to countless presidents and world leaders.

A critical lesson about purpose is that the emergence, the *generative* quality, of what is uniquely *our* life purpose is a core concern in the second half of our lives. There are many other core concerns, but this one must never be out of sight, particularly as we learn *how to grow old*.

What truly matters in life according to Viktor Frankl, Nazi concentration camp survivor and author of the classic book, *Man's Search for Meaning*, is not the meaning of life in general, but rather the specific meaning of a person's life at a given moment. "One should not search for an abstract meaning of life," Frankl advises. "Everyone has his own specific vocation or mission in life to carry out a concrete assignment which demands fulfillment."

Generative elders perform many "concrete assignments" in the world as guides, models, and mentors. But the most common assignment, ancient or modern, is to teach and to bring forth the voices of the next generation. The core assignment, today, remains the same: to help give voice to those voices. That said, not every elder is a teacher. To be both old and wise is a gift. The gifted elders are the generative elders—the ones about whom we can later say these magic four words:

"There was this teacher . . . who made all the difference in the world to me." We recall their generosity and the way they inspired us to find our own voice in the world.

Our experiences with gifted elders show us just how powerful this spirit of generativity can be. We marvel at their vitality, passion, and humor as they share stories that do more than merely offer a narrative of their lives—the most powerful tales provide insight into our common experience. We enjoy a roller coaster ride through personal history that takes us on a journey we embrace together. This is what it means to be a generative elder—magical, generous, funny, and wise. With such elders, we feel a kinship, an almost ancestral bond that enriches all our lives.

When generative elders share their stories, they are doing more than just recounting specific details of their lives' events. Their narrative gifts have more to do with savoring and saving the world. And beneath it all is their way of being in the world—combined with a spirit of generosity. In the way their faces lit up as they communicate, we see how generativity is not a philosophical or spiritual abstraction. We observe a deep wisdom in the lines on their faces and an inner strength in hands that have touched the world over many years. Generative elders are not simply telling us how to live, they are showing us, embodying the wisdom of their years. This embodiment, in its wholeness, is foundational to the elder role. It is what it means to be an archetypal *wise elder,* saving our communities by sharing our voices with our people. To do this is to more than merely inspire others though; it is also to truly savor the world.

Finding Your Voice

To grow old is biological destiny. But to become generative implies something more, an inner knowing that transcends aging. The generative elder is a person who knows about things that matter and at the same time knows how to savor the world. For generative elders, we observe that the final purpose of life is to die happy by teaching generously.

Not every elder knows how to transform his or her raw experience into this kind of wisdom. Not every elder automatically becomes wise and giving simply by getting older. In the elder's role there is a range of capacity and gifts—all the more reason why those who are able to teach are so important today. They have a critical role to play in the transmission of universal stories, core values, and moral legacies. Their purpose, should good health allow them to exercise it, is to inspire the younger generation so that the larger spiritual narrative of life can advance. Ultimately, each of us must, in our own way, offer our unique voice to the larger truths that embrace us all.

In *Wishful Thinking: A Seeker's ABC*, Frederick Buechner offers this: True joy comes from "the place where your deep gladness and the world's deep hunger meet."

Many people live in between the gladness and the hunger, neither savoring nor saving the world. They are not so unhappy with their current lives that they can't live with themselves. Neither are they so happy with their lives that they have no incentive to break free. They live in *limbo* — in the neutral zone between saving and savoring—committing to neither. Eventually, they might feel a growing sense of purpose, a feeling that there might be a greater mission or larger calling. Becoming generative in the second half of life becomes the ultimate test for whether we die happy.

In *Chasing Daylight,* the powerfully moving memoir of the last three months of his life, Eugene O'Kelly writes of the quest to find "perfect moments" with family members, friends, and colleagues in the limited time he has before death. He takes his doctor's prognosis that he has just three months to live as a gift that teaches him to live in the moment as he has never before. Although none of us would welcome O'Kelly's fate, we can't help wonder how different our own lives would be if we knew how precious little time we had left. Ironically, the belief that we have plenty of living left to do often keeps us from living as fully as we can.

The simple truth is that as we age, loss is inevitable. The longer we live, the more losses we will experience; it's an undeniable fact, clearly articulated by the Buddhist truism that life is suffering.

Yet no one, except in very dire circumstances, would consent to trading those losses for the opportunity to live a long and fulfilling life. The key then, in the second half of life, is not to avoid loss—which we can't do anyway—but rather, to discover better ways to deal with it.

Bad things will happen; that's out of our control. What is within our power, though, is how we react to those bad things. And to the extent that we can respond in a positive and generative way, we can mitigate the loss and continue to grow and evolve in the process.

One of the tools for responding effectively is what we refer to as "courageous conversations," conversations in which we reveal ourselves to one another honestly, in which we disclose our true feelings, our hopes and dreams, our fears and concerns. This doesn't mean we end up weeping in each other's arms; it does, though, require that we let those with whom we're communicating see who we really are, warts and all.

Being together with a group of one's contemporaries on safari in Africa for three weeks is a catalyst for courageous conversations. Talking about the weather gets boring after a while and you want to get down to the nitty-gritty with your fellow travelers. Another, more typical way that courageous conversations arise is when unexpected "wake-up calls" occur in our lives. When life-changing events occur— difficult times like death, illness, major job changes—we naturally are led to more meaningful discussions with friends and family. And it is often only through such discussions that we are able to make it through those difficult times.

We were driving through the northern Serengeti corridor when Richard reminded us about the power of courageous conversation. We were passing by a noble acacia tree in the shadow of a great rock on our way to the Soitorgoss passages where we would be spending several days hiking and meeting with Maasai elders. "See that tree there," he said. "That's where we spread my friend Bill Payne's ashes. Remind me to tell you that story tonight around the campfire."

And so, that evening, as we sat around under the stars, after dinner, Richard related the following story:

✣ Bill Payne was a dear friend of mine, a colleague, a fellow inventurer, someone who I bonded with the first time we met. His natural desire to travel and to grow had inspired his wife, Joan, to surprise him with a three-week Africa Inventure Expedition for his 50th birthday. And Africa, at least symbolically, had opened Bill's heart to old questions and new answers, new feelings. He was not carrying a heavy load full of regrets, but he did want to open his heart more in his relationships and to "speak his true voice with more courage at work, his creative expression, his unique contribution to the world." His heart told him it was time to face that which had caused him to shy away from life.

One evening, under an acacia tree on the edge of the Serengeti plains, we shared the edges of our lives. While witnessing the great wildebeest migration, we caught up with each other on the migration of our own lives. Like many of us who are in the second half of our lives, Bill wanted to share stories. He was not at a loss for feeling. He loved teaching, but most of all he loved sharing stories. He laughed, wept, and spoke movingly of the past and future. His central theme was: "I've lost my voice. How am I going to find it?" He wanted to create a life with a distinct voice he could call his own.

Over the years, as I have asked older adults what, if any, regrets they had, one theme has shown up over and over. The older adults interviewed said, "I wish I had taken more risks to be myself, to find my unique voice." Their greatest obstacle was their postponement—their choice to bury their authentic voice until later in life.

Bill's capacity for postponement was exhausted. Like many people, he had remorse about neglecting certain parts of his life in favor of others. Spiritually, he felt a great need to find something larger than himself to believe in. Bill's work increasingly needed to be an expression in the outer world of who he was becoming in the inner world. To feel whole, he needed to speak on the outside what was true on the inside.

As we sat together under the tree in Africa, Bill told me how excited he was about the upcoming year. He would keep doing what he was doing but change how and how much he did of it. He would travel less for work and focus more on relationships. Work travel had given him little joy in the past year. He would rekindle his joy by taking Friday off each week. With an intentional three-day weekend, he would spend more time with Joan and with close friends. He would change his relationship to relationships. He would, in short, find his voice and begin using it as never before.

Flash forward two years, back in Minnesota. I get a phone call from Bill in which he got right to the point "I have cancer," he told me, "a particularly bad kind—adenocarcinoma, a malignant tumor at the base of my esophagus—that will probably kill me. I don't know how long I have to live. I'm going to a specialist this afternoon."

The irony of throat cancer in a man who had been struggling to find his own voice was not lost on Bill. Was this the fate of having held one's voice inside for so long?

The painful news brought to the foreground the deep affection I felt for Bill. When we next talked by phone, in spite of his barely audible, raspy whisper, I heard his real voice come through almost for the first time. He spoke of his life and his imminent death; he talked about what he had accomplished and what he hoped to do in the time he had left, and he did so courageously.

When Richard related this story to us, we couldn't help but be moved. Our own conversations that night were deeper and more courageous than usual. We were reminded of the fragility of life and the importance of being grateful for the time we have. Above all, we were reminded of the power of courageous conversations and of the critical nature of finding and using our voices, especially in the second half of life.

Clearly, one of the requirements of discovering our voice is time—time to grow whole—to come face-to-face with the incomplete parts of ourselves. And to do that we must make friends with death.

Death is a powerful teacher. The wisdom of life can originate from brushing up against it. Squarely facing our own mortality, or that of others, forces us to take a fresh look and see reality. It can shatter old assumptions and generate new questions.

Ernest Becker, in his book *The Denial of Death,* claims, "The fear of death is the basic fear that influences all others; a fear from which no one is immune no matter how disguised it may be." Rollo May adds, "The confronting of death gives the most positive reality to life itself. It makes the individual existence real, absolute, and concrete. . . . Death is the one fact of my life which is not relative but absolute, and my awareness of this gives my existence and what I do each hour an absolute quality."

In the months following that fateful phone call, Bill confronted death squarely. During that time, he was poked, prodded, sliced, and scanned at length by medical specialists in Minneapolis and at the Mayo Clinic. He experienced weeks of radical radiation and chemotherapy. He worked with multiple therapies including massage, visualization, accupressure, diet, herbs, and meditation. He rejoined the Catholic faith, prayed, and attended healing ceremonies. And he revisited his personal purpose over and over, reminding himself to live on purpose every day. His purpose, "to bring forth harmony on the planet through the force of love," became his healing mantra.

Healing requires self-forgiveness of our inevitable crimes of unconsciousness. Bill said, "I was emotionally unconscious for 15 years! I denied the emotional me for 15 years. I'd been growing numb for a long time, and I really started to die inside about a year and a half ago. I started to see people as a group rather than as individuals. I even forgot people's names. My cancer is a mirror of my own integrity. In the mirror one morning I saw the enemy—me."

Bill and Richard began meeting more regularly to talk about purpose and meaning, all of which he filtered through his cancer healing journey. His cancer forced both to be emotionally vulnerable. It forced Bill to face the question, "Who are my friends and who is my healing support group?" He often said, "My cancer is not an undiscussable, yet many people close to me often are afraid to discuss it. It's curious how some people I felt close to now stay at a distance to avoid their fear or discomfort with my cancer. And people who I wouldn't expect show up!"

It was often hard talking to Bill. Sometimes Richard felt disconnected from Bill's struggle, almost like he didn't feel anything at all. Then, one day while driving in to work to meet with Bill, Richard's own grief broke loose. He sobbed all the way to work.

Most of us feel a need to be part of something larger than ourselves—to have something to live for. Awakenings, like cancer, call this to our attention. Elisabeth Kübler-Ross, who studied death and dying for many years, taught us that at the end of our lives we will ask, or be asked, three final questions: Did I give and receive love? Did I discover my own voice—my calling? And, did I make a difference?

In one of Richard's meetings he gave Bill a book entitled *A Year to Live* by Stephen Levine. The book offers a year-long program to help us learn to fully live before we die. Reading it himself, Richard was prompted to live as if he, himself, had only a year left. The experience of living this way for just one day informed and impacted his study of purpose profoundly.

Bill's healing journey offered him extraordinary insights into what he was living for, which became increasingly obvious. But the deepest insight was an increase in courage. When you live as if you have a year left, fear makes you too small. You live the life you've been postponing.

Bill's purpose—"to bring forth harmony on the planet through the force of love"—became his daily challenge, his reason for getting up in the morning. He said, "My struggle is a courage struggle. My cancer is about courage and voice—being in my heart and at the heart of things like relationships. My cancer is a mirror about living a life of integrity."

Living with integrity is an act of courage. But ultimately, what gives our lives joy is living in an integrated manner—being and acting in a way that is a bold expression of who we are at our core. When we feel integrated we feel, as Joseph Campbell put it, "the rapture of being alive."

Erik Erikson, whose classic work *Childhood and Society* depicted eight phases of maturity, believed that a later life task is that of achieving integrity. Integrity describes a person who has adapted to all of life and who has found a sense of wholeness.

Wisdom can occur when one is radically awakened. Bill's cancer pushed him to face his life squarely and summon his voice. If we are deficient in courage, no voice can be heard. His voice, however, was not the intellectual voice from his past. It was a new, soft, luminous voice tempered with love and the wisdom of compassion.

Bill died at his Minneapolis home in the loving arms of his wife, Joan. Richard's friendship did not end when Bill died. Some spiritual aspect of it deepened. The pain of his loss was the cost of deep friendship. Richard learned from Bill, as he has from so many of his true teachers, that compassion is the voice of purpose. Everything else pales in comparison. We do not need to accomplish grand things in order to show compassion for our friends, and the world. It is the power of compassion that we put into moments, day after day, that adds up to the power of a purposeful life.

The Sufi poet Rumi encourages us to think of our lives as if we had been sent by a king to a distant country with a special task. All of us are on a quest for something to live for. "You might do a hundred other things," says Rumi, "but if you fail to do the one thing for which you were sent it will be as if you had done nothing."

To be human is to search for "the one thing," the "invisible game." This quest is at the heart of the world's great religions and spiritual traditions. We're searching for the "one thing" that Rumi intimates and the rapture that comes with it. In the second half of our lives, this quest becomes essential. Purpose, something to live for, is the essence of our lives. Purpose determines how we spend our precious time and resources. Purpose energizes. Purpose motivates. Purpose structures and fills our day. Purpose is about holding a vision in life. Having purpose and vision is one of the most critical determinants of well-being in the second half of our lives. Purpose is essential because you can have it no matter how old you are, no matter how sick you are. Living on purpose in the second half inspires a voice of compassion. And Bill's voice stays with us, always.

Making Friends with Death

At a recent workshop, well-known Ashtanga yoga teacher Richard Freeman was demonstrating some variations on the pose known as "upward dog." After showing off several rather bendy versions, he illustrated one that featured little more than a raised head. "Don't be alarmed if this is all you can do," he said. "Eventually, we will all be reduced to this posture." And then he delivered a great quote: "Even if you practice yoga every day, you will still grow old and die."

Hard as it may be to accept this, it's true. Eventually, no matter what we do, no matter how well we take care of ourselves, we will all, in time, come to be no more—at least on this earthly plane.

Moreover, for most of us, our deaths will be preceded by a period of descent, during which our bodies, and perhaps our minds, too, will fail in any number of ways. Understandably, this is a scary prospect and not something we're likely to look forward to, but on the other hand, the inevitable path to our demise offers unprecedented opportunities for self-discovery and emotional growth.

As our days run out and the time remaining becomes more precious, we are likely to be more courageous in expressing ourselves with authenticity and wholeheartedness. We will probably have less patience for halfway measures and postponements. Chances are, we won't put up with situations or people that waste the precious moments we have remaining.

Everyone is familiar with the scenario of a person on his or her deathbed finally revealing some long-hidden secret or expressing an unexpressed sentiment for a family member or friend. While this makes for great drama, it also seems rather sad. Who wants to be dying before letting one's loved ones know they are loved?

It seems preferable, therefore, to get started on the project of personal revelation as soon as possible. We want to use whatever time we have left—especially as it dwindles—to say the things we've always wanted to say, do the things we've always dreamed of doing, and be the person we had always hoped we'd become.

And frankly, the only way to do that is to do it. We've got to accept the fact that our time is limited and use that to remove limits from ourselves. In this way, we do what Richard has called "making friends with death." We draw upon the knowledge that we're all dying—slowly but surely—to impel us forward to the full expression of who we are.

"Life is too short" goes the old adage, but that's only part of it. In addition, death is far too long for lives not to have been used by us to the utmost. A Buddhist admonition goes: "Let me respectfully remind you; life and death are of supreme importance. Time passes swiftly and opportunity is lost. Awaken! Take heed. Do not squander your life."

While the exact nature of squandering one's life may be open to interpretation, it's certain that one common feature would be the belief that it has been squandered. If we end up looking back upon our life and feeling that we've wasted it, then in all likelihood, we have. On the contrary, even if we haven't accomplished all that we might have hoped for—even if we haven't won a Nobel Prize and secured world peace and environmental sustainability—then if our assessment of how we've lived is positive, then what further proof do we need?

When Dave's mom was diagnosed with lung cancer at age 79, her doctor laid it on the line with her. "You're no spring chicken," he said, "so anything we might do in the way of treatment is unlikely to make that much of a difference."

"Oh hell," she responded. "I'm an old lady, and I've done everything I've really ever wanted to in life. My kids are grown and can take care of themselves without me. I'm going to enjoy the time I have left at home, on my couch, reading and relaxing, not here in the hospital being pumped full of drugs just to live a little longer."

Dave, who was with his mom in the doctor's office at the time, was devastated by the prognosis, but couldn't help but be even more moved by his mother's response. There was no denying she was right and her courage in choosing her own course of action was completely in keeping with her character.

Reflecting on that experience some years later, Dave says, "In so many ways, my mom taught me how to live; in that moment, and the months that followed until she passed away, my mom also gave me great insight in how to die."

A true expression of legacy indeed.

✍ *Letter to Live For: To a Departed Loved One*

If we're serious about making friends with death, we might do well to consider our connections to people we know who have passed on and what their lives have taught us about something to live for. Naturally, our own religious or spiritual beliefs will inform our understanding, but we can interrogate these views on a personal level through writing and reflection. In keeping with the project of writing "letters to live for," you might try crafting a missive to a family member or friend who has died. Doing so can have the effect of helping you to think about how death and dying informs our day-to-day living. It worked that way for Dave, anyway, when he wrote the following letter to his dad.

Dear Dad,

It's now been almost ten years since you passed away and not a day goes by that I don't miss you. At the same time, not a day goes by that I don't experience a part of you, in me, in the way I look at the world, relate to family and friends, and simply think and feel about nearly everything. Your influence on my life is deep and abiding and I thank my lucky stars that I had the great good fortune not to just know you, but to share probably the deepest connection—parent to child—that any two souls can share.

I delight in seeing your influence and temperament in my daughter, Mimi, and just wish with all my heart that the two of you had had more time to spend together. Still, somehow, perhaps channeled through me, perhaps by some inexplicable magic, you are reflected in how she is, in her cleverness, humor, and sometimes cantankerous manner.

I am proud beyond measure to be your son and hope that I am living in a way that is consistent with your compassion, integrity, and wisdom. I still feel I have a long way to go to be the man that you were, but I'm also confident that I had the best teacher and role model possible to show me the way.

You know, Dad, that I am extremely skeptical when it comes to assumptions about the afterlife and so on; so I'm not at all sure you're "out there" to receive this. However, I am certain that you are here, on Earth, in the world, through the great joy you spread to those who knew you when you were alive. I don't have any expectation of seeing you when I pass away myself; however, not only do I expect to see you every day that I'm here, I most certainly do.

Love always,

David

We encourage you to try this exercise yourself. Write a letter to a loved one who has passed on. See if you can find the words to say to that person what you've always wanted to say to them (even if you did when he or she was alive). You may find yourself connecting more deeply with parts of yourself that are sometimes hidden. We encourage you to put your whole self into the letter and feel what happens when you write authentically and wholeheartedly.

saving the world

Our age has its own particular mission . . . the creation of a civilization founded upon the spiritual nature of work.

Simone Weil, *The Need for Roots*

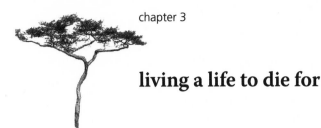

living a life to die for

Elephant in the Room

We've all heard the term "elephant in the room" used to refer to an obvious, but usually unspoken, issue that confronts us individually or as a group. When Dave teaches a philosophy class, the "elephant in the room" is always (especially later in the quarter) that the students haven't done the reading. Unless this core issue is dealt with, the class can't really proceed effectively. But even though it is an "elephant in the room," Dave often is inclined to ignore it. Of course, this never works. The "elephant in the room" always has to be attended to; like a real elephant, it can't be ignored except at great peril to anyone nearby.

The "elephant in the room" for many of us in the second half of life is that retirement—as conceived of traditionally—just isn't appealing, or to an increasing number of people, even possible. We want to be useful, contributing, connected members of our community. We want to make a difference in the world and we might need to continue to make a living to support our second-half needs. The question we can't escape, therefore, is how to do that.

In Africa one night, around the fire, Daudi told us a story to illustrate an "elephant in the room" when it comes to our roles as elders in our communities. And best of all, it's a story about actual elephants!

⤞)✲⤙ It seems, he says, that some well-meaning environmental group got the idea of re-introducing elephants into an area in South Africa where they historically lived but from which—due to poaching and land pressures—they had been eradicated. Since elephants live in matriarchal groups, it was decided that the most effective strategy would be to introduce a number of young bull elephants into the area.

Males live alone or in bachelor herds; being nonterritorial, mating success depends on size and weapons. Growth of the tusks continues into old age; seniors are therefore the biggest tuskers and do most of the breeding. Bull elephants annually cycle between a state of heightened readiness to mate called *musth* and non-*musth*. During musth, bull elephants have peak testosterone levels and are more aggressive. Older bull elephants—those at the top of the mating hierarchy—will allow the younger bulls who are in musth to mount female elephants in estrus as a means to prime the females for reproductive sex. Essentially the young bulls in musth tire out the females so the older bulls have a better chance for reproductive success when they eventually mate with the females.

Anyway, Daudi, tells us, what happened when these young bulls were introduced into this area of South Africa was that when they would go into musth, they would essentially go crazy. They rampaged about, terrorizing the local people, and even, in behavior that was unprecedented for elephants, stomped to death two rhinos. Nobody knew what to do to stop them and of course, nobody wanted to kill the elephants, although, for a time, this seemed to be the only solution.

Eventually, however, someone got the idea of introducing a few mature bulls back into the population to keep the young bulls in line. It worked perfectly. In just a couple of weeks, the mature elephants had corrected the behavior of the young bulls through a combination of behavior modeling and butt-kicking. What the young bulls needed was older, more experienced bulls to show them how to act—and to bust a few heads if additional persuasion was necessary.

When Daudi finishes this story, we are all nodding in recognition. We are aware that, as elders in our own communities, we are like those mature elephants who are charged with the responsibility of showing the young bulls the ropes. We realize that it is incumbent upon us to provide guidance and direction to the younger generation in our societies. We feel deeply the responsibility to model behaviors that will sustain the health and security of our communities. And, if the truth be told, we aren't entirely averse to doing a little butt-kicking if necessary.

We see ourselves as able to make meaningful contributions to individuals and groups throughout society. Figuring out how to do that is a bit more of a challenge. We know how to savor the world; our task now is to figure out how to save it.

Creating Our Future

Imagine this: You've made it successfully into the second half of life! You've gotten to a point in your life where your basic (and not-so-basic) needs are met. You have a place to live, food on the table, clothes to wear, reliable transportation. You can choose to do whatever work you want, or none at all. Basically, you are free to create your own future.

So what's next?

The situation described above is, in essence, one option that some fortunate people in the second half of life are now facing. And the question is the one many are asking themselves.

If we have real freedom to choose, then what will we choose to do with the rest of our lives?

As a life coach, Richard hears, on an almost daily basis, from new elders who find themselves in the position of having real choices for the future. Many of those who contact him are people who are considering retirement or who have just retired and are now wondering what to do with their lives. Some want to travel; others to study something they've always wanted to; others desire nothing more than to relax; but a common theme that also emerges is a desire to make a difference, somehow, to stay engaged with the world in some way.

Often, when he first hears from people like this, Richard advises them to take a moratorium—about two years—before deciding how to spend the rest of their lives. He hands out his business card and says to get back in touch with him in about 24 months, after the person has traveled, relaxed, and explored how it feels to wake up to a blank calendar and to-do list.

Not surprisingly, it usually is just about two years when Richard hears from them again. And typically, those he hears from tell him that they've enjoyed their freedom and have gotten the full-time recreation or exploration bug out of their system for now.

After recreation, these people are now ready for re-creation. They've had fun and are now hungry for meaning. It's at this point that Richard feels he can help provide some coaching direction.

And it's at this point that those who come to him are ready to do the generative work of connecting, in more meaningful ways, to the world-at-large.

In thinking about how to do that, we turn again to Africa.

✻❊✻ One of the best things about our walking safari in Tanzania is the element of the unexpected. It's taken all of us a few days to get there— that is, here, back to the rhythm of allowing ourselves to be surprised by whatever reveals itself. But now, about a week into our trip, we're all more or less willing to take things as they come, even if what's coming isn't what we expected. And as a result, we routinely enjoy experiences far richer and more authentic than any we could have planned for or predicted.

Today, for instance, our intention has been to walk from our campsite in the Nou Forest to an Iraqw—the local people, agriculturalists, who live by farming and the tending of goats and chickens—village about five miles away. There, our Land Rovers will meet us and whisk us off to our next campsite some five hours distant. The schedule, though somewhat flexible, is pretty packed; it's not like we don't have time, but it would be fair to say we don't have time to waste.

But about an hour into our walk, an opportunity presents itself that is far too good to pass up. We come upon a collection of eight Iraqw elders, sitting under a tree in a field a quarter mile from the road upon which we are walking. Daudi talks to them for a bit, having a discussion with the senior member of the group, a bald-headed graybeard with piercing black eyes. He is one of the chief elders for this village. He and his fellow elders are about to hold an informal council meeting just at this moment. Daudi asks if we can sit with them for a while until the meeting gets going. The man, who is referred to as Kuhamusmo, which means something like "elder representative," says we are welcome to join in, but just for a while. When the other members of the council arrive and the council gets down to business, we will be asked to depart.

And so, the rhythm of the day changes from action to reflection; instead of moving forward, we stop and sit down in the field with the assembled group of Iraqw men. There are eight of them: Kuhamusmo, who is 72 years old, five others who are around his age but somewhat younger, and then a couple of youths who have been invited to participate for two reasons: first, to witness how the elder councils operate and second, to run errands should the elders need someone or something fetched for them.

The pace of the council is very different than most of the meetings most of us have been to. In the first place, it's not as if there is an exact starting time or a precise list of participants. People show up as and when needed. No one consults a watch to get the meeting going. Rather, the conversation has a general flow that seems to be building as we sit there, talking quietly among ourselves.

At length, Kuhamusmo stands and addresses our group. Daudi translates his kind words of greeting. The elder welcomes us to his village and asks what brings us to this part of the world. Daudi conveys to him our purpose: We have come, as older members of our industrialized communities, to learn from elders in more traditional societies. We hope to draw upon the wisdom of experience from African tribal leaders to bring back new (and old) ideas for creating meaningful societal roles for men and women in the later years of their lives. And in doing so, we aspire to help manifest better connections between the young and the old in our parts of the world.

Kuhamusmo takes this all in and then conveys his appreciation for what we are doing. "What you are doing is vital," he says through our interpreter. "We, too, in our village strive to do the very thing you have come here to investigate. We, too, struggle to find ways to include our young people in the lives of our village and to train them for leadership roles of their own. So, we understand what you are seeking and commend you for your effort."

He says that in the interest of time, we can ask him two questions. So first, we ask him to describe how the meeting that is about to take place works and how people are chosen to be members of the group that is assembled.

Kuhamusmo explains that what is about to happen is a typical elder council meeting. Elders get together as needed to discuss issues that affect the village—land and water rights, planting and harvest decisions, agreements with other villages—and to settle disputes among village members. Taking part in decision making as an elder involves having the requisite experience and, quite simply, in showing up to participate. Today's meeting, for example, will begin when everyone who is involved in the outcome of the decision arrives.

The council is made up in his village of all men, but women are consulted when decisions will affect the entire village. In addition, women have their own leadership council to decide on issues that affect only the women in the community.

We ask Kuhamusmo to tell us about challenges his people face in maintaining a meaningful role for community elders and in preparing young people for their own roles in the ongoing life of the village. He surprises us by responding that, in his world, it is not so different than in our own. His people, too, face the difficulty of seeing that young people will carry on traditions and practices that have long defined the Iraqw. Outside influences, easy money, and the prospects of individual rather than collective success all tempt Iraqw youth away from their time-honored roles and responsibilities. Kuhamusmo admits that the elders in his community consistently bemoan the attitudes and behaviors of young men and women who are drawn away from what is traditionally expected of them.

This refrain is familiar, and we nod our heads sympathetically and talk among ourselves about this surprising similarity between our world and this one.

Kuhamusmo then turns the tables on us and asks us a question that leaves us all pretty much speechless. "Your people," he says, "have made great advancements in the world of technology and accomplishment. I see airplanes flying overhead that come from your countries many thousands of miles away. I see the cars your people make and the machinery you build, all of which is very advanced. And so I ask you: How could you let it get away from you? How is it that a people who are so technologically advanced, who have figured out so many complex things, have not figured out how to create a meaningful role for older people like yourselves and ensure that younger people respect and carry on the important traditions you value the most?"

We're stumped. We don't, at that point, have an answer. We look around at each other and shrug our shoulders. We laugh nervously.

Kuhamusmo understands our response without translation. He smiles rather sweetly, apparently commiserating with us. Eventually, he too shrugs, as if to say "What can you do?" Quite frankly, we don't know.

If, in spite of our technological prowess, we have let the traditional role for older people in society get away from us, then what are we to do, individually, and as a society? That question lingers with us and inspires many more conversations and questions on our trip and afterward.

In retrospect, some answers have emerged. To begin with, it seems critical that we create space for elders in our society to come together and discuss issues that affect us all. We'd like, by the force of our combined characters, to have greater influence in the world of which we are a part. And we'd like to extend that influence to include not just people like us, but younger folks who are looking for (or even not looking for) direction and guidance for themselves.

The challenge of establishing meaningful and relevant ties to youth seems especially critical. And yet, we recall our own younger days: While some of us may have occasionally trusted someone over 30, it was rare that we were ever taken with what some old person had to say. Our attitudes were well articulated in a passage from Thoreau:

> Age is no better, hardly so well, qualified for an instructor
> as youth, for it has not profited so much as it has lost.
> One may almost doubt if the wisest man has learned
> anything of absolute value by living. Practically, the old
> have no very important advice to give the young, their own
> experience has been so partial, and their lives have been
> such miserable failures, for private reasons, as they must
> believe; and it may be that they have some faith left which
> belies that experience, and they are only less young than
> they were.

Nevertheless, there is a powerful need, both on the part of older folks and younger people for connections to each other. It requires a certain amount of boldness, confidence, and willingness to take risks on the part of those of us with the experience to take the first step. There is a need here just waiting to be met. And it is in identifying such needs and then finding ways to fill them, that something to live for in life is found.

Leaving a Footprint in Time

"What am I living for?" "What matters?" "What footprint will I leave as my legacy?"

We may pose such questions at any stage of life, but in the second half, they matter more. As death looms ever larger before us, it's natural that we take increasing stock of our life. And as the day-to-day responsibilities we have shouldered for decades are made ever lighter, it becomes painfully—and joyfully—evident: we need a *reason* to get up in the morning.

When Dave's mom was in her late seventies, she put it well: "For my entire life, I've *had* to get up in the morning; now, the only reason I'll get out of bed is because I *want* to."

Having something to live for is the foundation of that desire, and at the root of that is the balance between saving and savoring the world. Essentially, it comes down to a matter of integrity, when saving wholeheartedly matches up with savoring authentically.

Fortunately, the "long view" that many of us develop at midlife and beyond serves us well in developing and sustaining the disposition to live with integrity, as we are better able to reconcile short-term desires with long-term ideals.

The Native American view of making choices with seven generations in mind embodies this spirit. According to this perspective, we are, in our daily choices, to consider the impact of our actions on seven subsequent generations. Doing so ensures that we act in ways that are sustainable and harmonious, thus establishing the core of our life's purpose and priorities.

When the community is weak or selfish, everyone stumbles through the seasons of life. When it gives generously, life flows with the power of purpose.

In some non-Western cultures, midlife is typically considered to be the time in the life cycle at which one begins to renounce worldly involvements and turn toward more spiritual practices. In the Hindu tradition, for instance, the idealized life cycle is equally divided into four parts: student, householder, hermit, and renunciant, or ascetic. Broadly, the first two stages represent savoring the world, those times during which our lives are more self-absorbed and focused on our own needs; the last two, saving it, when we turn inward to explore our own deeper spiritual yearnings, our generativity.

In the West, we would be well advised to accept the reality that what we valued in the first half of life will change in the second. It is only natural that as we edge closer to having, as Shakespeare put it, "shuffled off this mortal coil," that spiritual considerations will take higher priority.

Whatever our metaphysical speculation about the afterlife, we can be sure, at least, that as human beings, we live on after we're gone in other people's memories of us. It's no wonder, then, that we crave connections not only with our contemporaries, but also with people at every stage in the life cycle who we have touched and been touched by. This is the essence of "living a life to die for."

If a community "desires to live spiritually," wrote psychiatrist Robert Coles in the conclusion of his book, *The Spiritual Life of Children*, "then it looks upon the ancient [person], who belongs both to the past and to the afterworld, as its embodiment."

From time immemorial, until just the last century or so, the older members in society passed on wisdom and knowledge to those who came after them. At the same time, there was never any doubt that stronger members of the society would care for the weaker, young and old alike.

Through these natural sharing connections, then, a person's legacy organically evolved. By the time you reached later life, your influence ran throughout your community. This again is one of the reasons we marvel at generative elders: Through their connections with their people, there is no doubt that their spirit will be carried on, for some part of them is in each and every one of those whose lives they touch.

Traditionally, this sort of connection happens both informally and formally, through daily interactions as well as more structured initiations from one stage of life to the next. Consequently, the influence of elders on those who followed was fairly predictable. Nowadays, though, it's much harder for those of us in the second half of life to be assured that we are reaching forward through the years to make a difference in the lives of those who follow.

One thing is certain, though: All that we do pass on is all that we are. The authentic and wholehearted expressions of our being are communicated—intentionally or unintentionally—to our children, grandchildren, and younger colleagues, students, and friends. We may envision ourselves as sending one message or another, but, in the end, the only message we can send is through the life that we lead, the way that we are.

Richard had this brought home to him quite poignantly in a piece of writing that his 36-year-old son, Andrew composed. In it, Andrew talked about one aspect of his father's legacy.

My dad was a runner. For most of my childhood, there was a nook in the scary basement near the heating oil tank that held a smelly assortment of New Balance shoes, t-shirts, bandanas, and for most of the Minnesota year, mittens, hats, and jackets.

The "jogging stuff" took my dad on nearly daily excursions around Lake Harriet in south Minneapolis. The three-mile door-to-door round trip was the trade route for him, and a seemingly impossibly long distance to my 7- year-old legs. Rain, shine, sleet, blizzard, 20° below zero or over

100°, he was on the road, to the lake and beyond. I didn't realize it at the time, watching his dedication and commitment, but I was learning.

We had big front bay windows that faced the street, and, a few blocks away, the lake. I began waiting for him. I would stare down the street, inadvertently memorizing every house and tree, until he came jogging into view, familiar in his cream and silver track suit. When he appeared, with frost thick on his full beard, I studied him. Watching his even stride and kick up the hill, I was learning.

I could barely finish the run in the President's Physical Fitness Test, hating every second of it. My dad, meanwhile, was training for his third Twin Cities Marathon. "Training" was a foreign concept to me. At my age, you either had the innate ability, or you were picked last. I was often the kid stuck in deep right field. A marathon, to me, was a distance akin to our annual trip to see Grandma in Honolulu.

Watching the marathon pass by our door was a ritual of cold fingers, donuts, and Dixie cups of water. We lived between miles 7 and 8, and would watch every year with our neighbors, shouting as the leader cruised past the television van, and then the thousands of everyday runners, like my dad, who flowed past as a stream of anonymous athletes I could never hope to be.

Then, like fireworks going off, there was Dad, running in his blue nylon shorts, with his bandaged nipples, and a red bandana on his head, just as he looked approaching our front window countless times.

I was proud of him. "My dad's a marathon runner, what's yours do?"

My father and I are alike in almost every way. We have the same physical structure, appearance, manner of speech, stance, and above all, viewpoint. We even have similar work. I realize now, with 30 years of hindsight, that I was not just absorbing how to run, or the value of exercise and health, I was learning how to hold commitments, how to challenge myself, and how to have fun each day. I was learning how to be who I would be one day. I was watching my future self.

I call myself a runner now, too, and even have a few marathons to my name, including the Twin Cities. My family moved from the house on the race route long ago, but when I ran past it after mile 7 that year, my dad was home, cheering, and looking proud. I was so caught up in the run that the change of roles didn't hit me for a few days, but it left a lasting impression.

I know what my daily run means to me, but funny, I've never asked my dad why he went to the lake everyday. I'll bet our motivation is the same, as are so many other things we share.

As I watched my dad run, I was learning.

Stories like Andrew's remind us that wherever we walk (or run) through life, literally as well as figuratively, we are leaving a footprint that others may follow. It's incumbent upon us, therefore, to move into the second half of life with an awareness of the wisdom—or lack of it—we are passing on.

As people age, they develop what gerontologists call "interiority"—the increased internalization of past and present experiences. They spend more time reflecting on the past in order to seek meaning and understanding in life. Those who develop interiority trust themselves to determine their values and priorities rather than looking outside of themselves for validation.

One of the ways we do this is by noticing our voice in others. Insofar as we are able to sense the spirit of our words in the lives and lessons of those we have touched, we are better able to understand ourselves. This, of course, requires that we refrain from merely standing aside and letting the future take care of itself. We have to engage with the world and commit to living generatively.

Erik and Joan Erikson, well-known developmental psychologists, call this need to look within "ego integrity." They believed that those people who do not achieve ego integrity end their lives in despair. Such individuals are not able to look over their accomplishments, relationships, and work and find purpose. They're the people who reach old age and feel, "I didn't make a difference!" Or "My life had no meaning!" They're the people who die inside long before they physically pass on.

To avoid that fate, we need to successfully navigate the transition from a life of external focus, to one that is more reflective and introspective. Paradoxically, the way to do this is to develop a save-and-savor the world point of view. Strange as it may seem, when our concerns are less self-absorbed and more supportive, we're able to see ourselves more clearly. A less self-absorbed perspective enables us to take a more objective viewpoint on the meaning and purpose of our lives. By developing real compassion for others, we ultimately take care of ourselves.

Living by Giving

The classic film comedy, *Groundhog Day*, illustrates a series of experiences many of us may have at many times during our lives—upon going away to college, following a divorce, when our kids finally leave the nest—times when major life transitions force us to re-evaluate why we're here and what we're doing with our lives.

But perhaps the analogy is most apt to retirement, when the scenario depicted in the movie may seem eerily familiar to men and women in the second half of life.

In the film, Bill Murray plays Phil Connors, a pompous, jaded, and egotistical Pittsburgh-based television weatherman, a guy so self-centered that he can refer to himself, without irony, as "the talent."

As the action opens, Phil is preparing reluctantly to head—along with his one-person camera crew and neophyte producer—to Punxsutawney, PA, to cover, for the fourth year in a row, the annual Groundhog Day festivities.

Phil makes abundantly clear his distaste for the entire proceedings, which he considers cornball and hick and far beneath his abilities, which, he is sure, are soon to take him away from the podunk city in which he is based and off to a national network.

But when a freak snowstorm traps Phil and his crew overnight in Punxsutawney, everything changes.

Phil awakes in his room at the bed and breakfast to what he thinks is the next day, but which he soon finds out is February 2nd—Groundhog Day—all over again.

At first, Phil thinks he is experiencing *déjà vu*; he convinces himself that he must have imagined the day before and does his best to bluff his way through what becomes an increasingly disorienting experience. But when once more his trip back to Pittsburgh is prevented by the blizzard and again, the "next" day, he wakes to the same Sonny and Cher tune on the clock radio, he's unable to deny the strangeness of his experience.

Phil thinks he is losing his mind; he even visits a neurosurgeon and a psychologist to see if they can help him—which they can't.

Such disorientation is not unlike what many folks experience in the early days following their retirement. They wonder "who am I?" "What is this place I'm living in?" The familiar looks unfamiliar, the unfamiliar utterly strange. Many seek help, but many, like Phil, find such assistance not all that useful.

Phil bemoans the fact that the day that's repeating is not the one he would have chosen. At a bowling alley bar with two down-and-out drinkers, he recalls a day spent in the Virgin Islands on a beach with a beautiful woman, eating lobster and drinking piña coladas. "That was a pretty good day," he says, "why couldn't I get that day over and over?" Again, this may feel familiar to many retirees who had expected their lives to be different than what they are experiencing. Some would have expected to have a bigger nest egg; others to be more involved in the lives of their children and grandchildren; still others to be fully retired instead of still needing at least part-time work to generate income.

In what may be the movie's best moment, Phil muses aloud, "How would you feel if you were stuck in one place, and every day was the same, and nothing you did mattered?" His drunk companion pauses, burps, and responds, "That about sums it up for me."

Soon though, Phil comes to terms with his situation. The realization that there will be, for him, no tomorrow, is totally liberating.

At the wheel of his drunk friends' car, Phil speeds through downtown Punxsutawney, crashing into parked cars and mailboxes, being chased by the police and narrowly missing being run over by a freight train. When he's arrested and thrown into a jail cell but awakes again the following morning to the same Sonny and Cher tune in the same bedroom once more, he jumps for joy and begins to live out one fantasy after the next, from casual sex, to bank robbing, to playing at being Clint Eastwood.

Again, this is probably not at all unlike what some period of retirement is like—at least in spirit—for many people. Playing golf as much as we like, traveling to all those places we always wanted to visit, doing things we weren't "permitted" to do as working folks; that's the fantasy that becomes real for those who have the means and the medicine to do so.

For Phil, though, this period of self-absorption eventually wears thin. A time comes when the fun is no longer fun—it's just more of the same old thing. He sinks into depression, sitting on the couch at the bed and breakfast in his pajamas, drinking bourbon from the bottle, watching *Jeopardy* and answering perfectly all the questions he's heard endless times before to the amazement of the assembled guests.

Once more, this may seem familiar to those familiar with retirement. Many people do hit a wall just like Phil. "I can only play so much golf," they say, or "You've seen ten foreign capitals, you've seen them all." Pure pleasures can cease to be purely pleasurable; it's not uncommon to see folks who were once extremely excited at the prospect of having no daily responsibilities deeply depressed by the lack of them.

Phil tries to kill himself—unsuccessfully of course—but the poignant analogue here is with the alarmingly high rate of suicide among the elderly, especially men.

Finally, though, after who knows how many identically dark days, Phil discovers the secret of something to live for. Instead of focusing on his own pleasures and needs, he makes it his mission, as he goes through one Groundhog Day after another, to help others and give of himself in their support.

He learns how to play the piano so he can make beautiful music for the citizens of Punxsutawney; he catches a kid falling out of a tree; he saves a man from choking with a timely Heimlich maneuver; he materializes out of nowhere with a hydraulic jack and spare wheel to assist a trio of old ladies whose tire has gone flat.

And in fact, this change in attitude and behavior ultimately proves to be Phil's ticket out of the hell he's been experiencing. When at last he has learned to both save and savor the world, he awakes on a day that is different than all those he had experienced before. Finally, today is tomorrow.

This feeling of something to live for is what we all desire, no less during our retirement years than at any other time. But what may be more critical as we age is that in order to find it, we must find it through giving to others. Just as Phil's life was stagnant when all his attention was focused on himself, so we, too, find singular self-absorption to be a dead end. The film *Groundhog Day* reminds us of a truth we all know implicitly: Without something to live for, life is not worth living and only by living with the concerns and needs of others at heart can we live in a way that sustains us day after day after day.

In some ways this sounds like a serious challenge, or at least one that requires us to engage in deep soul-searching, but as a matter of fact, it is, at least in principle, quite easy. The idea was articulated beautifully by a friend of Dave's, Alex, who, in his late forties, transitioned out of his career in the high-tech industry to open a bicycle repair shop serving a low-income neighborhood that had never previously had such an establishment. He said he decided to "give away what he loved," which in his case were his well-developed skills in bicycle repair, human resources, business management. His shop, over time, has become a kind of community center, where people from all walks of life congregate to talk about and work on bikes, but also to share stories, music, and just time together.

Alex has also taken under his wing a number of neighborhood kids, helping them to develop not only bike repair skills, but more importantly, real life skills for coping with the sort of challenges in living we all face.

And all this has happened quite naturally, without a great deal of strain on Alex's part, primarily because he is doing something he authentically cares about and which flows wholeheartedly from his own character. It seems almost miraculous, but in fact, nothing could be more common and natural. Throughout history, it has been the most common role of all for older folks to mentor the young, introducing them to the skills they will need to succeed in their environment. Only in our modern world, with its stratification of ages and economics, do we consider this unusual. But when we look at traditional societies, like the tribes we were privileged to visit, for instance, we see clear examples of such mentoring every day.

The question for new elders in the contemporary world is how to pass on our legacy—our wisdom, talents, and money—in a manner that can be received and learned from. Of course it is possible—even if rather rare—but we can pave the way if we are able to clearly articulate our hopes and dreams for the next generation. We can do this in many ways; one that many people have found effective is the ethical will.

Living an Ethical Will

People who live the longest and happiest lives appear to be those, like Phil Connors, who eventually develop ego integrity and positive interiority. By finding their own satisfaction through giving to others—individuals, community, or a cause—they continue to have hope and find meaning and fulfillment in whatever they do, no matter how aged, physically challenged, or limited they become.

Such mature people often engage with life in deeper ways than when they were younger. Paradoxically, they tend to be, while active and energetic about their lives, relatively accepting about the inevitability of dying. They have made friends with death while simultaneously living and leaving their legacy.

Another film, *The Ultimate Gift*, an adaptation of the best-selling novel by Jim Stovall, illustrates this quite dramatically. In his will, billionaire Red Stevens forces his grandson, Jason, to learn the value of helping others before the boy can claim his vast inheritance. Along the way, the young man learns that there is more to life than money, receiving a series of gifts, in the form of lessons that his grandfather, played by actor James Garner, wants to be remembered for.

Garner's character did what more and more people in later life are doing: making sure that the estate they leave behind does more than simply build a bank account. Instead, we want our bequests to become a force for good, in our children and grandchildren's lives, and in the world. These days, it's not how much money we give but why we give it and what will be done by those who have received whatever gifts we bestow, financial and otherwise.

This idea is embodied in what is known as an "ethical will," a document that, in contrast to the traditional will, tells your loved ones what you want them to have, lays out for them what you want them to know or to be.

An ethical will can be anything from a letter to a memoir to an artwork, even a video that enables you to communicate with your survivors the essence of what you see your authentic legacy to be. Often, it provides a personal history (or series of important stories) and messages to loved ones about the values you hope they carry on, Above all, an ethical will has to do with the nonmaterial gifts such as moral legacy, blessing, and life lessons you wish to leave to family, friends, and the world-at-large.

An ethical will helps us harvest the wisdom of the first half of our lives to more generatively shape the second half. Maggie Kuhn, the indomitable founder of the Gray Panthers, urges us to do something similar in what she calls a "life review." A life review inspires us to realize the ways we have coped and survived in the world through the stories by which we define ourselves.

By recalling these stories, a life review can give us new passion and energy. It not only helps us embrace our past history, it challenges us to picture what we want the rest of our life to look like, as well. Like an ethical will, a life review can broaden our vision at any age and can serve as a critical tool with which to approach life.

Dan Wakefield, in *The Story of Your Life,* says "To draw a map of our spiritual journey is to look for the experiences and changes, the turning points, triumphs and crashes, dark nights and mountain peaks we have traversed to become the kind of person we are."

Whatever the form, the purpose of an ethical will (or life review) is to provide a means to pass along a legacy to others and to find meaning in our own life—in other words, to help us save and savor the world. It hearkens back to the closing line in the poem "The Summer Day," by Mary Oliver: "Tell me, what is it you plan to do / with your one wild and precious life?" In an ethical will, that plan is laid out.

Dr. Andrew Weil strongly advocates the power and the purpose of writing an ethical will. In his book *Healthy Aging,* he writes, "You can and should write an ethical will. You can choose to share it while you are alive, or leave your thoughts for your loved ones to share after you are gone. Regardless of your age, an ethical will can be an exercise that makes you take stock of your life experience and distill from it the values and wisdom that you have gained. You can then put the document aside, read it over as the years pass, and revise it from time to time as you see fit. Certainly, while an ethical will can be a wonderful gift to leave to your friends and family at the end of your life, its main importance is what it can give you in the midst of life."

Richard had the privilege of interviewing Dr. Weil on the final stop of his book tour for *Healthy Aging: A Lifelong Guide to Your Physical and Spiritual Well-Being.* In the green room, before stepping on stage before a sold-out house at the Fitzgerald Theater in St. Paul, Richard and Andrew spent a couple of hours talking about healthy aging and purpose.

Dr. Weil spoke of his belief in "unchanging essence"—that part of a person that is unaffected by time. As a pioneer in integrative medicine, he believes that good medical care must address whole persons, meaning bodies, minds, and spirits. "Unchanging essence," said Andrew, was "spirit, the nonphysical core of our being." He believes, as we do, that it is possible to look at the world through scientific and spiritual lenses simultaneously, and that authentic well-being ensues when both spheres—the physical and non-physical—are addressed.

Richard and Andrew opened their conversation that evening with the question of purpose: "Why is it important to have something to live for?" Dr. Weil highlighted the importance of having a reason to get up in the morning and the role of an ethical will in healthy aging. He stated that "an ethical will helps us discern what we will leave behind, our legacy, but just as important, it gives direction to the rest of our living."

He shared some excerpts from his own ethical will and concluded by saying, "It helps me accept the fact of my aging." (You can read his ethical will, at age 62, in the last chapter of *Healthy Aging.)*

Richard prefers the term "anthropology" to ethical will, a term he draws from Viktor Frankl. Anthropology refers to our core assumptions about the origin, nature, and destiny of human beings. It covers our answers to the core questions, "Where did I come from?" "What am I to do here?" and "Where am I going?" Our answers to these questions form our philosophy of life, our anthropology, and equip us with our own way to shape and guide our lives and work. A life of saving and savoring the world necessarily confronts these questions authentically and wholeheartedly.

Here, then, are some excerpts from Richard's anthropology, as he, also at age 62, reflects upon becoming a new elder.

I believe...

There exists a loving God—a Source that created humans and all beings to fulfill specific purposes in a mysterious and evolving universe.

Meaning is not invented, but discovered; our purpose in life is to give moment-to-moment meaning to life through self-transcendence and service; purpose joins self and service into something to live for, a reason to get up in the morning.

Every individual being is born with distinct gifts that are given by God and called into expression from cradle to grave; we are called for life to give our gifts away; jobs end, roles end, but callings never end.

Being human means being free; the essence of humanity is freedom; this awareness instills hope: The freedom to choose and change is ever present in our lives.

Death gives instruction to life; the wiser we become, the clearer we understand that compassion is the core lesson we are here to learn; compassion is the authentic inner urge we feel to give our gifts to others; when we give—we have something to live for.

The ultimate purpose of life is to die happy; the way to die happy is to be thoroughly used up when we go—to live our lives for the sake of worthy purposes we feel wholeheartedly about.

Richard's anthropology is the belief system that grounds his life. It is the essential message he hopes his life stands for. And it is the message, ultimately, he would like to have spoken at own memorial service.

Richard's colleague at the University of Minnesota's Center for Spirituality and Healing, Rachel Freed, was introduced to the notion of the ethical will by a rabbi who was facilitating a woman's study group. Taken by its validity to her life—she was separated at the time—Rachel drove home and raced to her computer to write love letters to her children. She says, "I was so open and vulnerable and I had a lot I just wanted to tell my kids."

In her work at the time, Rachel was speaking about and distributing the powerfully healing *Heartmates* book and program that she had created for heart patients and their families. The ethical will concept seemed like a parallel idea, so she quickly developed the book and seminar entitled *Women's Lives, Women's Legacies.* She recalls, "Everything I saw began to look like 'legacies,' so I started filling a manila folder with articles and stories." She took classes on the ethical will over a three-year period and started building a curriculum. "I'm an advancer of ideas," she says, "not necessarily a creator of them. But this voice in my head kept saying to me 'Turn this concept into a healing tool for women.' And my rabbi teacher one day said, 'Just do it! It's an important niche!'"

So, Rachel did just do it, starting with a small group at the Shakopee Women's Correctional Institution. She still recalls, with emotion, working with the "Women Lifers" group and hearing their desperate desires to be remembered by their children and families. Rachel says, "Many of them will die in this institution. Yet they have the exact same emotional and spiritual needs for leaving a legacy as the wealthy, middle-class women I teach in my other classes."

The Shakopee facility is located near Minneapolis, far from the southern roots of one of Rachel's most faithful "lifer" students. This woman's plight was heartrending; she would never see her children or hold her granddaughter Sophia again; and the weight of it was crushing her spirit and will to live. Rachel, though, helped her develop an ethical will practice of writing one sentence to Sophia every single day. Suddenly, almost overnight, the woman felt significant, that she could matter and in some way have a role in her granddaughter's life. Rachel says, "Watching women find their voices and their values is thrilling! It gives me something to live for! I was a therapist for 30 years and I didn't realize how exhausting therapy is. But what happens in this process is 'transforming instructions into blessings.' Instructions aren't received very well, but blessings are. When people really 'get' how blessed they are, they want to bless others."

Clearly, there are as many reasons for writing an ethical will as there are wills; the unique experience for the writer is an important part of it.

Every one of us needs to carefully review our lives, discern what our hearts draw us to, and then choose this path with all our energy. Martin Buber makes this point when he recounts what Rabbi Zusya told his followers shortly before his death: "In the world to come I shall not be asked, 'Why were you not Moses?' whispered the rabbi, 'I shall be asked, 'Why were you not Zusya?'"

Our challenge in the contemporary world is not to try to live up (or down) to some externally imposed idea of a life to die for, but to find within ourselves the authentic enthusiasm (literally, "to be filled with God") to make our own personal contribution to saving the world.

And unless we want to be a martyr, we must also savor it.

If we do not take care of ourselves, sooner or later, we will not be able to, or we will resent taking care of others. Saving the world must be grounded in savoring the world or it just won't work.

It is in this spirit that we must serve others. The key is to keep that enthusiastic spirit alive, not just in our place of worship, but in the places where we live and work and love.

Martin Luther King, Jr., had more than just a dream—he had a dream and he lived it! During his famous speech at the March on Washington in August of 1963, he shared his dream with the world. Nine times he mentioned his dream during that unforgettable oratory, the last the most eloquent expression of all, "I have a dream that one day every valley shall be exalted, and every hill and mountain shall be made low . . . and the glory of the Lord shall be revealed."

Every time we hear or reflect upon King's words, we feel their stunning power, in part because they are an embodied expression of his deepest purpose—coming directly from his soul, translated into heartfelt language, so that every single person in his audience could feel the power of his legacy.

Not everyone can touch the world in that way, but like Dr. King, each of us can dream. And each of us, through making those dreams live beyond our own time, can live a life to die for.

ꙮ *Letter to Live For: Ethical Will*

Writing an ethical will is a matter of taking a stand for what you believe in most strongly. It's a way to articulate your most deeply held beliefs for others to hear or see. In a sense, it's like casting out a message in a bottle to the future, only it's one that you can live today, as well. We encourage you to take the opportunity to craft your own ethical will. In addition to Richard's anthropology, here's Dave's ethical will.

> I, David Shapiro, being of (relatively) sound mind and body, do hereby bequeath the following to my daughter, her children, and their children for as long as any memory of me shall remain in the hearts and minds of those who live on after me:
>
> Above all, I hope I am leaving you a world that's a little better place than I found it—and even if I'm not, I hope I am at least leaving you an aspiration for doing that. I have tried to live in a way that spreads compassion and care and if there's anything of value I can leave behind, I think it would be the desire to be kind to others—again, even if I've not always succeeded in fulfilling that desire.

I leave to you a love for ideas and discussion and some tools, I hope, for communicating with other people and yourself. I humbly bequeath to you a love for solitude and reflection as well as a deep affection for good company and vital dialogue.

I grant to you and yours free reign to your recollections of me as both a model of how to be and how not to be. I offer that paradoxical advice: "don't take anyone's advice" in hopes of encouraging independent thought tempered by wise counsel of those you respect.

The one lesson I learned (again and again) in my life that might be of value to you (on the off chance you haven't already gotten it) is that, in the end, all that really matters in our time here on Earth is how we have treated other people. All our own projects, problems, and possessions are simply sidelights to the real meaning of life, which is to connect meaningfully with other human beings. As long as we do that, we have had a life well-lived.

I pass on to you courage, independent-mindedness, and ingenuity. I hope I have shown you some examples of getting yourself into unexpected fixes and how to get out of them with some grace and humility. I grant to you, insofar as I am able, free reign to make lots of mistakes and a willingness to apologize for unintended slights, hurt feelings, and other misfortunes resulting from carelessness, enthusiasm, and just plain self-centeredness. Take from me the knowledge that you are a good person all the way down, even if you do, as we all do, trip up as often as not.

Above all, I leave to you a world of which I am no longer a part—at least physically. And in doing this, I hope, above all, I have left you with all you need to make do in such a

world. Let my most enduring gift to you be the ability to
live happily and healthily without me around. If as Socrates
said, "the aim of those who practice philosophy in the
proper manner is to practice for dying and death," then I
hope I have, in doing so, given you ample opportunities to
practice for my death and to carry on in your own life and
the lives of those who follow you, as well.

Here again, is an opportunity to write from the heart. Try crafting a version of your own ethical will. It needn't be anything overly complex or expansive. Simply try to articulate the lessons and learnings you would like to pass on and be remembered for. It may work more easily for you to do an "anthropology" like Richard or a more typical ethical will like Dave. In either case, we encourage you to share your writing with a close friend or loved one. You may be surprised how profound the effect of communicating your ethical will to another can be.

why purpose is good medicine

One should not search for an abstract meaning
of life. Everyone has his own specific vocation or
mission in life to carry out a concrete assignment
which demands fulfillment.

Viktor Frankl

Expecting the Unexpected

✣ On a walking safari in Africa, you walk on well-worn century-old
trails, through savannahs and fields of tall grass, across fast-moving
streams on slippery fallen logs, and over tree-covered plains teeming with
wildlife of all sizes. And that's what we've been doing all morning.

Our group has covered half a dozen miles since breakfast in a
variety of terrains. We have seen thousands of birds and animals of all
sizes. We have experienced mist and rain and now, around noon, sun that
beats down fiercely from overhead. In short, it has been a perfect day for
a hike and we are all, though tiring, totally into it and completely up for
more of the same this afternoon.

But just as we begin to set a course through the low acacia trees
that mark our path to our afternoon's destination, Daudi points out a
sight that changes our plans for the day.

Strung between two trees at about shoulder level is a loop of wire,
the strong steel kind that farmers and ranchers around the world use to
build and mend fences. And in that loop, hanging by the head, its body
butchered and covered with flies, is the carcass of a zebra.

This is the work of poachers, Daudi explains, who string up these snares in the dead of night to catch and kill unsuspecting animals as the four-legged beasts make their way to nearby watering holes. The animal before us is relatively fresh; it can't have been dead more than 12 hours or else, thanks to hyenas and vultures, there would be nothing of it left anymore. Therefore, there are probably, conjectures Daudi, other such snares around here and, more likely than not, the poachers themselves may be nearby.

We spend the next several hours searching around for more traps, finding and dismantling about half a dozen. It's not exactly what we'd planned for our day, but it somehow seems more important than heading to the river we'd been on our way to reach. Instead, after taking down the snares we find, we head back to the running water source a few miles away and sure as Daudi has predicted, run across a clearing in the bush where the poachers have set up camp.

The danger, at this point, cannot be overemphasized. The poachers are desperate men, in a desperate situation. They almost certainly carry weapons and, as Daudi emphasizes, would not hesitate to use them, especially out here in the bush, miles from any official authorities or rule of law.

We have run across many dangerous animals out here—lions, hippopotami, Cape buffalo—but none is nearly so dangerous as the human animals now on the horizon.

Maintaining our distance so they don't see us, we make note of the exact location of the place and then secretly head back to our own camp some miles away to contact the rangers in the vicinity. Again, this hasn't been at all what we've been planning to do but no one questions it's the right thing to do.

That night, sitting around the fire talking about our day, we share a sense of energy and purpose that has sometimes been missing when we've been savoring more purely safari pursuits. While we don't deny that our foray into wildlife protection wasn't what we'd had in mind for the day, we readily agree that it was a better way to spend the day than we had anticipated. It's not as if our actions today have saved the world, and indeed, some of us are somewhat ambivalent about having turned in the poachers, who arguably have turned to this illegal activity because no other options are available to them, but still, we have, in a small way, put our whole selves on the line in support of a cause we believe in. And that feels good, even though it wasn't what we initially set out to do.

We planned our day to mostly savor the world, but ended up doing a bit of saving. And in doing so, ended up feeling whole and alive—savoring the day even more.

Money, Medicine, and Meaning

The aliveness we felt that evening in Africa flowed from a sense of having done something useful; in our daily lives, we're all familiar with the glow that follows from meaningful accomplishments. But unfortunately, for many people, the opportunities to do something worthwhile may feel limited in life's second half.

Vital aging in the second half of life depends on the three M's: Money, Medicine, and Meaning. "Money" is obvious: We need to have the financial wherewithal to provide for ourselves and, with any luck, to be able do some of the things—travel, take classes, enjoy life—we may have put off until the "right time." "Medicine" refers to health; and as often noted, older adults today are, by and large, healthier than at any other time in history. "Meaning," however, is the missing key for many people. They have the money and the medicine, but they just don't have a powerful sense of purpose—a reason to get up in the morning. Money and medicine will not inform our spirits and make us whole. While they can be quantified and counted, it is the knowledge of what can't be seen—the invisible game—that we need for authentic vitality.

The good news, though, is that, far more than the other two, money and medicine, meaning is the one factor we're most in control of. We can count on finding and having meaning because we can choose it. It's always within our power to choose our reason to get up in the morning. The money and medicine may run out, but meaning will sustain us our whole life long.

Most of us can recall with a sense of deep fulfillment some time or another when giving our gifts to another—an individual, organization, or cause—felt more like receiving, when another's happiness was our own. These are the experiences that are indelibly etched on our memories, the ones by which we define ourselves. And what all these experiences tend to have in common is that they all emanate from a sense of purpose, a sense that we are doing in life what we were somehow meant to do.

There are multiple pathways to purpose and meaning in life. We can seek out elders to guide us, engage in spiritual practices, undertake any variety of service to others. Life itself will give us meaning through positive and negative experiences. Viktor Frankl's life shows us how to turn suffering into meaning; in many other examples from the world of philanthropy, we see how abundance transforms to meaningful activities. It's up to us to be open to these breakdowns and embrace them wholeheartedly as breakthroughs.

If we choose to be among those who live their lives with purpose and meaning, we will discover something special about life and about our own lives. We're each distinct, an experiment of one. All of us have special and different gifts. A purposeful life comes from a free and generous bequest of those gifts upon the world.

Meaninglessness and Medicine

One undeniable fact of life is this: We are all growing older. As long as we're alive, there's nothing we can do about that. We can, however, radically influence our experience of the passing years.

How we perceive the process of aging profoundly influences our health and well-being. Is aging a blessing or a curse? A decline or an ascent? A necessary evil or an opportunity to transcend? Our answers to these questions are key because they help shape our vitality and our destiny.

Being purposeful during the second half of our lives is one of the most critical determinants of mental, emotional, physical, and spiritual well-being. Social science research increasingly demonstrates this striking fact which, not surprisingly, is deeply grounded in all major religious traditions worldwide—articulated perhaps most clearly in the admonition to love our neighbors and our enemies as friends. For example, in a nationwide study of older adults at the University of Michigan Institute of Social Research, researchers found that elders who gave assistance to others experienced significantly greater feelings of well-being than those who did not provide such support to others.

In another study, retirees were categorized into four groups: givers, receivers, givers and receivers, and neither givers nor receivers. At the end of six months, the "givers" had significantly better health than any of the other groups. People who neither gave nor received help from others experienced the worst physical and mental health over time. Health and well-being are thus associated directly with being the sort of person who gives of him or herself to others.

We suffer physically when our lives are devoid of meaning—for example, working at something that does not engage us wholeheartedly. More people suffer heart attacks on Monday mornings than at any other time during the week; researchers have concluded that this is because so many people face a week of work that sucks the meaning from their lives.

And it's not only our hearts; our backs are literally breaking with the stress of meaninglessness, too. When Richard consulted with the Boeing Company, he observed a near-epidemic of back pain among its Seattle employees. And predictably, white-collar office workers suffered as much disabling pain as blue-collar workers who regularly lifted heavy loads. The best predictor for back pain turned out to be job dissatisfaction, not physical exertion.

Having something to live for, beyond our own self-absorption, is associated not only with better health, but also with greater longevity. Givers don't just live better, they live longer, too.

Any major transition or life change can challenge our sense of purpose and meaning and negatively impact the quality and/or length of our lives; however, having something to live for can help to reduce the stress of transitions by challenging feelings of uselessness that contribute to worries and depression. Focusing on something larger than our own problems and issues and channeling our energies in those directions will distract us from self-absorbed concerns.

Robert Butler, founder and chairman of the International Longevity Center in New York City, writes in his provocative book, *Why Survive?* about the "retirement syndrome":

> People who retire do not automatically develop declining
> mental and physical health. What social science studies we
> have, indicate such generalizations tend to be a fallacy. Yet
> there are clinical indicators that some individuals are badly
> affected. . . . Men and women who are otherwise perfectly
> healthy sometimes develop headaches, gastrointestinal
> symptoms, oversleeping, irritability, nervousness, and
> lethargy in connection with retirement. These conditions
> may manifest themselves before retirement takes place;
> they can heighten with the confusion of roles, activities,
> and changes in the structure of life that develops at
> the time of retirement; they worsen if one does not
> find a satisfactory lifestyle and work supplements after
> retirement . . . Without purpose, a sense of inadequacy can
> evolve, and apathy and inertia.

One of the greatest healers of our time, Carl Jung, claimed that after age 35, every emotional crisis is a crisis of meaning. It is unnatural to disengage from purposeful activities and withdraw from societal involvement as one grows older. Disengagement is not part of normal, vital aging. Our hunter-gatherer ancestors didn't; their contemporary descendents, the Hadza don't, and we shouldn't either. There is solid evidence that a disengaged, self-absorbed life can lead to mental and physical ailments and even more compelling evidence that a life of engagement with others and the world can contribute to longevity and well-being. Purpose, in other words, is good medicine!

Meaninglessness can make us sick; but a sense of purpose—something to live for—can make us well.

Deep relationships are one aspect of purpose; consequently, they are good medicine. They are a doorway into another dimension of life—a dimension that typically becomes more apparent to us only in the second half of life. If it were easy to open this door into authentic, wholehearted relationships, we would do it early in life. All marriages would be until "death do us part," and we would all live happily ever after.

Unfortunately, it doesn't always work this way. Growth through the life cycle is neither continuous nor smooth. We lurch forward and stumble back with the inevitable crises of life.

Two people fall in love and get together, but individually they may not be two whole people. In the second half of life, according to Robert Johnson, what we are ultimately seeking with a partner is the inner truth of our own soul. He writes, "What we seek constantly in romantic love is not human love or human relationships alone; we also seek a religious experience; a vision of wholeness."

Seeking wholeness is the invisible glue that bonds long-term relationships together. It's the spiritual connection we observe when one person dies; we often see that person's partner die shortly thereafter.

Dr. Bernie Siegal found that he could do a good job of predicting which of his cancer patients would go into remission by asking this question: "Do you want to live to be 100?" Those with a deep sense of purpose in their lives answer yes, and they were the ones more likely to survive their illness.

As families are increasingly spread across the country, aging parents and their adult children face difficult choices about where each should live out their lives. We have models, though, that give us insight and direction and from them, we learn how we might proceed in our own lives, for instance, Abe and Mollie Kaye.

Friends and family said that Abe and Mollie went together like lox and bagels. For 74 years, they were partners, through life and in death. Abe died at age 93; twelve days later, at 90, Mollie followed. Their deaths came just two years after they had reluctantly moved from Passaic, New Jersey, where they had lived all their lives, to Leisure World, a retirement community in Southern California, where, in their waning years, they could be closer to their children.

Their final years were bittersweet, as they balanced their homesickness and failing bodies with their acceptance of being cared for by their family. Beverly Kaye, Abe and Mollie's oldest child, said "Every single solitary day they missed their friends; they missed Passaic. They talked about it all the time. But they knew in their hearts that they needed the care of their children."

What really mattered was that Abe and Mollie had been together all those years. Beverly continues, "Mollie was very weak, and she said to me many times—before Abe died—'I'm ready to go.' My father knew that if he died first, that would release her. As my mother sat through his funeral, she had a calm about her."

Since purpose—something to live for—is hard to measure, we have no quantifiable gauge of how many relationships come this far on their journey. After all the studies are done, we are still left with an essential mystery. But, those of us in the second half do not need statistics to tell us what we already know: that long-term relationships can provide us with a sense of meaning that sustains us through our days. Deep, lasting connections with others are based on truly savoring and saving—the seeds of something to live for. The maturity, of which saving and savoring are the vital ingredients, provides the capacity to move through the inevitable crises to a deeper kind of love—a love that provides meaning and purpose throughout our lives.

How Can I Help?

Perhaps no one has made the point that health is primarily a product of meaning than psychologist and Nazi concentration camp survivor, Viktor Frankl. In his classic *Man's Search for Meaning,* Frankl describes how, in the concentration camps, those who lost a sense of meaning or purpose in their lives quickly gave up and died. By contrast, prisoners who had some sort of reason to get up in the morning, even it was simply to share a crust of bread with another, had a much better rate of survival.

One of the things we discovered in our interviews for this book is the power of the question, "How can I help?" Ram Dass and Paul Gorman wrote an entire book on this question, detailing the stories of ordinary people who provide selfless service to others, and how serving in this way transformed their lives.

Why is service to others such a positive force in people's lives? Why is having something to live for such a powerful motivator? Ask the question, "How can I help?" and we are instantly transformed through the gift we offer to another.

We believe that one of the best ways to develop a purposeful life is to put yourself in the presence of people who embody and evoke such transformative energy. This was recently brought home clearly to Richard when he met Emmanuel Ofosu Yeboah, featured in the film *Emmanuel's Gift.* Emmanuel was born in Ghana, with a deformed leg and consequently extremely slim life expectations. In his culture, disabled babies are considered a curse on their families and are normally put out in the street or left in the woods to die. But Emmanuel's mother refused to follow the norm. She named her baby Emmanuel—"God within you"—and instilled in him a sense of purpose and value. Refusing to beg, he was able to become self-sufficient in a society where the disabled (almost 10 percent of the population) are abandoned, shunned, and hopeless.

To show his countrymen that disability doesn't mean inability, he pedaled a bike donated by the American group, Challenged Athletes Foundation, 379 miles around Ghana—pedaling only with his left leg. Now able to stand on two feet, thanks to an operation and a high-tech prosthetic, Emmanuel works vigorously to ensure that opportunities are made available to all physically challenged Ghanaians.

Thanks to the documentary, *Emmanuel's Gift*, thousands have been able to share Emmanuel's emotional and uplifting story, and he has garnered worldwide recognition and awards for his work and impact on others. Richard shared a conference stage with Emmanuel recently and interviewed him about his own "something to live for." Emmanuel shared the view that it was in helping others that he most clearly helped himself. When he worked to provide care and opportunities for physically challenged people, his own physical challenges seemed to go away. By helping to make others more able, his own gifts became empowered.

In *Emmanuel's Gift*, we get a window into Emmanuel's purposeful approach to life: When the neighborhood kids won't let him play in their soccer games, he saves up enough money from shining shoes to buy his own ball. The kids can use his ball, but only if they include Emmanuel.

Relying on his grit and charm, he finds odd jobs to help support his mother, but remains dismayed that all around him, disabled people are sitting in the streets begging. Emmanuel decides to change all this—to give them something to live for—by changing how disabled people perceive themselves and how others all across Ghana view the disabled, as well. He resolves to lead by example.

With the prize money from his awards, Emmanuel returned to Ghana to set up his own foundation to promote educational scholarships, wheelchairs, and sports opportunities for disabled youth. Now running for a seat in Ghana's Parliament, he articulates a clear vision of how this core trio of school, assistive technology, and sports will give disabled kids a chance at life—in short, something to live for.

It may sound a bit much for the lurking cynic within us all, but Emmanuel is for real—a modest, yet confident soul who will find his way through any suffering, quietly but purposefully. He is testimony to the oft-quoted adage that "one person can make a world of difference." Toward the end of the film, one of Emmanuel's friends casually remarks that Emmanuel reminds him of Martin Luther King or Nelson Mandela—and the remark does not seem at all overblown.

Emmanuel's experience hearkens back to a central tenet in Viktor Frankl's philosophy of "logotherapy," which is that suffering—physical and/or emotional—can be a source of meaning and purpose in life if we can shift our attitude toward that suffering. Frankl wrote, "We must never forget that we may also find meaning in life even when confronted with a hopeless situation, when facing a fate that cannot be changed. For what then matters is to bear witness to the uniquely human potential at its best, which is to transform a personal tragedy into a triumph, to turn one's predicament into a human achievement."

If we are unable to change a predicament—think of Emmanuel's life prospects at birth or Frankl's experience during the Second World War—we are challenged to change ourselves. The philosopher Rene Descartes took it as a foundational principle of behavior "to endeavor always to conquer myself rather than fortune, and change my desires rather than the order of the world." This is the attitude that gives rise to the personal discovery of something to live for.

At the same time he met Emmanuel, Richard also made the acquaintance of Rudy Garcia-Tolson, one of the leading young lights in the Challenged Athletes Foundation, an organization committed to providing training opportunities and funding for disabled atheletes. Rudy, who was born with rare multiple birth defects—a combination of crippling pterygium syndrome, a club foot, webbed fingers on both hands, a cleft lip and palate—lives by a simple motto: "A brave heart is a powerful weapon."

As a gold medalist in the Paralympic Games and a member of the U.S. Paralympic Elite Team, Rudy works tirelessly to raise money and awareness to ensure that other physically challenged athletes have the same opportunities he did. Rudy's words to Richard echo those of Emmanuel. He said that by working to help other athletes with similar challenges, his own challenges seemed diminished. By helping to reduce the suffering of others, his own gifts were strengthened.

Contrast this attitude with how often we adopt a victim-like perspective on our own misfortunes—usually far less unfortunate than what Rudy, or Emmanuel, or Frankl experienced. Their life stories demonstrate to us that developing something to live for requires that we change our focus from wallowing in our own misery to providing support to others; in this way we simultaneously save and savor the world.

And again, the link to purpose cannot be overstated.

Our purpose is the specific outer expression of the gifts that the world asks of us. Purpose is what gives us a reason to use our gifts and a way to use them.

Richard refers to his own purpose as "helping people discover the power of purpose," and he uses it as a brand identity on his business cards. The purpose came first, the business practice second. He was lucky enough to uncover his purpose early in life. This happens occasionally, and perhaps more often with rare individuals like Emmanuel

Yeboah or Rudy Garcia-Tolson, but most of us go through many trials and errors before clearly identifying something to live for.

In recent years, many fine thinkers have written about finding purpose in life—and especially later life. Richard Bolles, author of the best-selling *What Color Is Your Parachute?*, suggests that we ask ourselves how we are best suited to serve humanity. He calls it our "mission," and speaks of it as a "vocation"—a calling from God.

Bolles suggest that we think of our lives in terms of a symphony, with four different movements. There's the early stage when we're an infant, the stage when we're learning, the stage when we're working, and then, the fourth movement, what used to be called retirement, that he refers to now as "fifty-plus." This fourth movement can have different characters; for example, in Tchaikovsky's *Pathetique* Symphony, the fourth movement just sort of drifts off and peters out; that's why, says Bolles, it's pathetic. By contrast, in Beethoven's *Eroica* Symphony, the fourth movement is heroic. And what makes for a heroic fourth movement, in Bolle's view, is the sense that we're really a part of a symphony orchestra and that each of us is a player with a unique and important part to play. In other words, we've identified clearly our purpose and are contributing to the greater symphony of life by expressing it.

Those who write about personal purpose or mission, despite different nuances in language, seem to agree on at least one critical point: Our purpose is not something we create out of the blue. Rather, purpose is to be uncovered, through life experiences and reflection upon them.

This point of agreement is critical because it suggests that uncovering something to live for is an act of discernment rather than creation. Our purpose is our own unique, one-of-a-kind form of both saving and savoring the world, essentially written into our personality as if via genetic code. Frankl writes, "One should not search for an abstract meaning of life. Everyone has his own specific vocation or mission in life to carry out a concrete assignment which demands ful-fillment. Therein, he cannot be replaced, nor can his life be repeated. Thus, everyone's task is as unique as is his specific opportunity to im-plement it."

We pursue our purpose because we must. We pursue it because at some deep level, we know it is essential to staying alive, or, as in the Bruce Springsteen lyric, everybody has a "hungry heart."

Keeping the Main Thing the Main Thing

A joke in the upper Midwest is that Minnesota is the Land of 10,000 lakes and 10,000 treatment centers. Fortunately, for many who have passed through one of those numerous rehab facilities, there is a wel-coming place of worship and good feeling, a congregation in the Twin Cities, known popularly as the "Recovery Church."

In 1940, more than 1,100 people worshiped at Central Park Church in downtown St. Paul. By 2000, before the Reverend Doctor Jo Campe arrived, the congregation had shrunk to 11 elderly members. Today, hundreds of people stream in and out at all hours, every day of the week, and 95 percent of them are involved with some sort of 12-step group.

In the 1990s with a doctorate from Princeton Theological Semi-nary, "Pastor Jo" was a rising star in the United Methodist Church. During that time he was senior pastor of one of the largest congrega-tions in Minnesota. With a TV show, a radio show, and a loyal follow-ing, Jo had everything—with one exception: sobriety.

The charismatic preacher was an alcoholic, and no one knew. At night, he would drink himself to sleep in the parsonage, where he slept alone because his wife had left him. Hitting rock bottom, he checked himself into a treatment center after waking up from a blackout next to a loaded shotgun. He had intended to commit suicide.

Pastor Jo left that program recalling, "No one was comfortable talking to me; no one that is, except those who had been in 12-step programs." He eventually landed at the Central Park Church with a vision to create a five-day ministry for St. Paul downtown workers and government employees. But then Alcoholics Anonymous members starting attending and encouraging Jo to start a "recovery worship service." Forty people attended the first service; 100 showed up at the second one. Today, members and nonmembers come from throughout the Twin Cities. Each week, 1,500 people attend Alcoholics Anonymous, Narcotics Anonymous, Overeaters Anonymous, Sex Addicts Anonymous, Al-Anon, and other support groups.

Richard and Jo have been friends since college days when Richard spent his last dime to bail Jo out of jail, on a drinking-related charge, during the first week of school! Since starting the Recovery Church, Jo has invited Richard to speak with his congregation on several occasions. Following Pastor Jo before an audience is no easy task. At six-foot-five, with both the build and the history of a championship swimmer, Jo fills the sanctuary with the vitality and presence of a man who has finally discovered his purpose in life. The first time Richard spoke to the congregation, Pastor Jo opened with, "Hi, I'm Jo, and I'm an alcoholic." The congregation instantly responded with, "Hi, Jo!"

Richard recalls taking a long, deep, nervous breath and wondering what he might possibly have to say to the alcoholics, addicts, former and active prostitutes, judges, mortgage bankers, executives, school teachers, and "normies" (people without addictions) eagerly staring back at him. As he approached the sanctuary, Jo smiled and whispered to him, "You don't have to be a drunk to come here, but it helps! Just share stories about purpose. They get it!"

Brokenness brings people to the Recovery Church. Purpose helps heal them.

The Recovery Church blends 12-step principles with Christianity to inform and define its entire ministry. All of the church's events relate to some aspect of recovery. Stories of purpose and hope are given every Sunday and members sign up months in advance to share their tales. In the middle of his talk, Richard asked each member of the congregation to turn to the person next to them and share his or her own stories "on purpose." He recalls, "The place was electric with real drama and real listening. It moved me very deeply."

Pastor Jo's own purpose guides everything he does. He is fond of saying that his purpose is to "keep the main thing the main thing." And the main thing for Jo is "to bring the message of God's love to all people in recovery." He says, "We don't know what we're doing, so we just try to stay out of God's way." Getting out of God's way hasn't been an easy trip for Pastor Jo, but, with His help, the Recovery Church shows why purpose is good medicine.

Uncovering Something to Live For

As the Buddhists remind us, life is suffering. Suffering seeks us out; while we may try to insulate ourselves from it, suffering cannot be avoided. And when something happens that causes us to really suffer, our world can be shattered. The day-to-day concerns that typically occupy us become petty and irrelevant. But life goes on and when we eventually reclaim ourselves, we are changed forever.

We can be transported into a larger context in which we see what is truly important, worth living for. How we respond to suffering can be seen as the true measure of the power of purpose, for if our purpose is strong, our response can be positive and life-affirming. We can see these situations as openings to growth and healing, as good medicine.

Lynn Fielder lives in a body with Parkinson's Disease. Richard met Lynn when they were both speaking at the San Jose chapter of the American Leadership Forum of which Lynn is an alumna. Her story is an inspiration to all who hear her.

"The clock ticks," she relates, "And I open my eyes on another day on which I am the intimate witness to the struggle between my brain and my body, the brain and body of a 45-year-old woman, wife, and mother, with Parkinson's Disease."

"My body is stuck to the bed and uncomfortable. I have not moved a muscle during the night. I want to lounge a few minutes and ask my husband, 'How was my night? Did I keep you awake with vivid vocal dreaming? I don't remember!' But I abandon such congenial chit-chat because I am on a mission. My body is giving me two contradictory messages: 'Get to the bathroom right away!' And 'I'm not moving!'"

Lynn's paralysis is due to the fact that her brain is running on empty when it comes to dopamine levels. It is thought that at least 80% of dopamine-producing brain cells are gone when the first recognizable symptoms of Parkinson's appear. Lynn was diagnosed in her early thirties, right when her adult life was taking off—she had a newborn baby and a career on the rise.

Forced into premature retirement, she says she is giving new meaning to the term "stay at home mom." "When my daughter has to be picked up from school," Lynn says, "I often have to tell her I won't be coming until my body unfreezes and I overcome my temporary paralysis."

Lynn depends upon a handful of life-giving pills every three hours to regain her mobility. She knows the medications will eventually lose their effectiveness and, unfortunately, this drug tolerance occurs every evening. Without dopamine, her brain can't tell the body to move. Lynn says, "This causes a phenomenon akin to a union strike; labor isn't budging despite what management says."

The clock ticks. She's still not moving and she still has to get to the bathroom. "In anticipation of this dilemma," she says, "I have stationed my recently acquired electric wheelchair next to the bed the night before. With the help of the grab bars on the bed and the wheelchair, I finally reach the bathroom—my sanctuary. The second thing I do there is take my pills and wait; wait 20 to 60 minutes for the drugs to take effect and when they do, it is glorious.

"Until that occurs, my morning is 'all about me.' My husband gets himself and our daughter ready for work and school. We are lowering our expectations of what I will accomplish at home because we know I will have numerous cycles when I am unable to function effectively—walk, swallow, balance, speak clearly or audibly. I frequently resort to my new hobby, jewelry-making, which can be meditative and when I lose myself in it, the time passes more endurably, especially during the insomnia. Or, I might share my sleeplessness with other people with Parkinson's who can be found on the Internet any time of the day or night."

After Lynn related her story to participants at the American Leadership Forum, she went on to inspire them to train for the up-coming wilderness adventure they were to share together in the High Sierra of northern California. On her own wilderness adventure several years ago, she mesmerized the entire group with her ability to do it all—climb, trek, camp out—and was instrumental in it being a life-changing experience for all involved.

Lynn typically closes her talks by thanking audiences for the opportunity to speak with them and with a reminder of how important it is for her to be out in the world, telling about her life and the life of others afflicted with Parkinson's. "I describe my 'struggle,' but I am conflicted about this word. It is a struggle, but I don't want to evoke pity or a 'poor dear' response. I am holding on dearly to the important life lesson to take what comes 'as is' and with as good an attitude as I can muster. I can have a bad disease and a bad attitude or a bad disease and a good attitude; the way I respond to it is really the only thing I can control. I work to stay in the present. I don't focus on 'why me?' because the answer is always the same: 'No known cause, no known cure.'"

As Lynn's story shows us, the meaning and purpose of life is a life of purpose and meaning.

If we can identify our purpose, like Lynn Fielder does, we can be proactive in living it, and life, in spite of inevitable suffering, will be more fulfilling.

Our purpose is the moment-by-moment, day-to-day expression of our gifts. It gives us something to live for, a reason to get up each day. An important aspect of Lynn's wisdom is her intuitive sense that purpose is good medicine. She senses that serving others will somehow serve her own healing journey.

Simply being present, with deep listening, is one of the most healing and life-altering practices we can undertake to discover, define, and express our purpose. Richard has found, in his coaching practice, for example, that when he listens deeply, his silence is a more powerful expression of his purpose than his speaking. Purpose, in the form of deep presence, is good medicine, too.

Some people have always lived to be very old, but never before have so many lived so long, so healthily, and with such a strong sense of possibility. Many millions of people around the world can now look forward to 25 or more years after retirement age (whether they choose to retire or not) of decent health and vitality. Harry "Rick" Moody, Director of Academic Affairs for AARP, and a philosopher and scholar on the subject of aging, describes these millions as the "wellderly," as distinct from the afflicted "illderly."

In our fifties and sixties, it is typical that we feel more powerful stirrings of that paradoxical desire to both save and savor the world. We're aware that we're moving from "middlesence" into "elderesence," and want to do something important in the time we have left but want to do it on our terms and in our time.

Something is shifting in our bodies, which is difficult to understand or name—it's almost a second adolescence, but the territory is uncharted. We may feel alone in experiencing a sense of unrest. We may worry that every ache or pain is a sign of something much worse. Most likely, we're waking up to our own mortality and struggling with the inevitable, yet new, sensations of our aging bodies.

"What I recall most about turning 60," says Richard, "is that it was a time of mild, but continuous unrest, sort of like turning 13, but different. This 'elderescence' brought with it a new sense of urgency. Unlived parts of my life were calling for attention. I was wrestling with the purpose question at a new level of experience. I felt like I was crossing over into elderhood somehow. But there was no ritual, no sign of passage."

The late Betty Friedan, in *The Fountain of Age*, called this mood "crossing the age divide." Gail Sheehy coined it as a "passage into the age of integrity." And Daniel Levinson termed it the "late adulthood transition." We call it uncovering "something to live for." Regardless of its name, however, what matters is allowing the underdeveloped or hidden parts of our self to emerge and evolve. By doing so, we revitalize ourselves with the good medicine that is purpose and integrate ourselves more fully into this next transition that life has to offer. We grow whole, not old.

In his book, *From Age-ing to Sage-ing*, Rabbi Zalman Schachter-Shalomi points out that the current model of human development based on aging ends in a state of personal decline, where a person becomes less engaged with the world toward the end of life. But it doesn't *have* to be this way. As an alternative, he proposes the model he calls "sage-ing," in which older adults become "spiritually radiant, physically vital, and socially responsible elders of the tribe."

Our culture clearly yearns for new models such as Schachter-Shalomi's "sage-ing." Individually and collectively, we are inspired (and sometimes a little jealous) of how older people have rediscovered their something to live for and achieved great things in their seventies, eighties, and nineties, and even beyond.

Nelson Mandela celebrated his 89th birthday by joining with other "sages"—Nobel Peace Laureates, former Presidents, other governmental and societal leaders—to form a "Council of Elders" dedicated to fostering peace and resolving global crises. The event made world news as a vital Mandela took the stage, accompanied by an aide and leaning heavily on a cane.

"How God must love South Africa to have given us such a priceless gift!" former Archbishop Desmond Tutu told Mandela. "You bowled us all over by your graciousness, magnanimity, and generosity of spirit!"

The Elders, all poster-children for something to live for in the second half of life included, besides Bishop Tutu, former U.S. President Jimmy Carter, former UN Secretary-General Kofi Annan, Indian women rights campaigner Ela Bhatt, former Norwegian Prime Minister Gro Harlem Brundtland, former Chinese envoy to the UN Li Zhaoxing, and Nobel Peace Prize winner Muhammad Yunus.

These Elders will "support courage where there is fear, foster agreement where there is conflict, and inspire hope where there is despair," said Mandela.

Could there be any clearer expression of the role most of us seek later in life? Any clearer example of what it means to both save and savor the world?

Most of us want to be elders in a council of elders like this in later life. We want to assume a meaningful role in fostering the continued success of society, to give back to future generations, to "claim our place at the fire," in the second half. We want to live our deepest hopes and purpose for ourselves, our families, and the larger world, authentically and wholeheartedly. We find something to live for by leaving our mark upon the world.

ᕦᕤ *Letter to Live For: To A Wise Elder*

For this *Letter to Live For,* we encourage you to write to an elder who has shown you what it means to live wholeheartedly and authentically, who has been a model to you for saving and savoring the world. For our sample letter, we offer one to an elder of the Hadza tribe we met while on safari in Tanzania. His name is Kampala, and while we will introduce him more fully in subsequent chapters, suffice it to say here that at more than 90 years of age, he embodies a vitality and connectedness to his land and people that we could only marvel at. Our experiences with Kampala convinced us that having something to live for is possible at all ages, just so long as those deep cross-generational connections are maintained.

Dear Kampala,

We write to share how deeply we were inspired by you and the lessons we learned from your presence.

First, you are an elder ideal; you embody the spirit of wholeheartedness and authenticity to which we aspire. Having seen you—connected to your people, your land, and your way of life—makes us fully understand the possibility and reality of vital aging.

We carry an image of you in our minds that illustrates the simultaneous nature of saving and savoring the world. We see you providing mentorship and direction to the younger members of your tribe in their search for a bee's nest dripping with larvae and honey. You tease and cajole them while making sure they have the skills and awareness to succeed. And when the honey is found and secured, you are first in line to sample it with gusto.

We marvel at your storytelling ability and—like the tribe members listening—hang on your every word, too.

You make the past come alive and draw us into deep connections with our shared ancestral roots.

And this, perhaps, gets closer to what we really want to communicate: Above all, what you have made us aware of is our shared humanity. Although we come from vastly different worlds, being with you has enabled us to see that we are all one people. We all share the lineage begun thousands of years ago in the land you and your tribe still populate; we are all hunter-gatherers; we are all, at the end of the day, Hadza.

We reveled in your stories and storytelling—epic tales about the creation of the world to simple accounts of your day's adventures. You've illustrated for us a life that draws upon the essential saving and savoring that we all naturally seek out. We've seen that gleam in your eyes when you tell stories or pass on traditional teachings to others and we've responded, as have all those around you, with a sense of illumination in our own selves as well.

Probably, above all, it is your compassion—for others, for the land, for a way of life that is sustainable—which inspired us. You embody that compassion. You are, in the fullest sense, a model for us of putting your whole self into the second half of life.

Kampala, we are honored to have had the privilege of spending time in your presence. We will carry your message onward throughout our lives and hope to be able to pass wisdom on to others we meet, as well.

In closing, let us then just say *tutaonana baadaye*, we will see you later—in this world, we hope, or another, surely.

Take this opportunity now to write a *Letter to Live For* to a wise elder in your own life. Offer your gratitude for the positive guidance and/or impact that this person has had on your life. Put your whole self into the letter and don't hesitate to send it!

finding your way

connecting with others

How long the road is. But for all the time the journey has already taken, how you have needed every second of it in order to learn what the road passes by.

Dag Hammarskjöld

✳️ *What Does Life Expect of Us?*

In a grassy clearing beneath the shadows of massive rock formations, we're gathered together to form a circle, all 14 of us, middle-aged and older men on this "inventure" safari through northern Tanzania. It is the second-to-last night of our two weeks together and we have begun to reflect on what it will be like to return to "civilization" and our "real lives."

Richard reminds us that "re-entry" can be a challenge; people who have not been on a trip like this may find stories about and accounts of our experience boring, off-putting, or simply meaningless. If we arrive face-to-face with loved ones, co-workers, and family and begin regaling them with tales of our African adventure, they may recoil, shut down, or otherwise ignore us.

So the key advice we are given is to practice "your story, my story." Let others tell you their stories before telling yours. Rather than inundating our audience with a deluge of details from our trip, we are cautioned to create a two-way flow of stories that allows us to drink in the experiences of those who haven't shared ours.

Richard tells us to identify for ourselves people who will "get it" when we talk to them and set up a time to converse with them, perhaps taking a walk together or even better, sitting by a fire and chatting. Ideally, we'll share no more than two or three stories, each one crafted so as to reveal something about ourselves as much as about the African experience.

While these recommendations are intended specifically to assist us in re-engaging with our lives upon returning from an intense trip abroad, they also function as helpful advice for how to connect with others in our day-to-day lives. In particular, such guidelines are useful for us, as elders, in coming to reveal and align ourselves with younger people in everyday life. Too often, we are of the opinion that age has given us unique wisdom that will answer every question those younger than us may have. But as it may turn out, we haven't even identified what those questions are!

One of our guides, a man named Palanjo, who represents for our group a model for an enlightened elder, puts it best: "Wisdom is giving the right message to the right person at the right time."

And that's a message which is right for all of us, right now.

Survival for What?

For much of our lives, this question sounds ridiculous because we don't really have a choice in the matter. For most of us, paid work is essential to our survival; if we don't work, we don't eat.

But in the second half, when our refrigerator is stocked and our basic needs are met, then something more than mere survival must be at play. Many of us work—and more to the point, hunger for meaning-ful work—long after the time we are required to by physical need and well past the time society has traditionally expected us to.

As a life coach, Richard has the opportunity to ask his clients this basic question, "Why work?" in a variety of contexts and at many different stages in people's lives. And he remains struck by the number of people who answer that all their hard effort and long hours are devoted to the goal of gaining the freedom not to work. In short, their answer to "why work?" is "so I don't have to."

In their book, *The Millionaire Next Door: The Surprising Secrets of America's Wealthy,* authors Thomas Stanley and William Danko report that many self-made millionaires launch their careers with the goal of accumulating enough wealth to quit working and start savoring life. One of the millionaires profiled called his stash "go to hell money"—a safety net that empowered him to walk away from work anytime he wanted. For him, money bought the time and freedom to savor the world.

This strategy fascinates and confounds us because we often see wealthy people who do not know what to do with the freedom that their money buys them. Many of the self-made millionaires studied by Stanley and Danko did not obviously enjoy their fortunes. Their life-styles remained essentially the same after they became rich as before. The experience of really savoring life eluded them.

Some people with "go to hell money" become so addicted to the money-making game—and the buzz from winning—that they can't give it up. Increasing their fortune becomes a goal in itself but one that paradoxically is never attainable. For some, making money becomes a surrogate for the personal fulfillment associated with helping family, friends, and the community. But a poor surrogate it is.

The difference between making a living and making a life is immense. Sadly, people who focus their lives solely on the former, on acquiring wealth, often end up living a life of regret. They confront an ailment with no single cause or cure. Some call it social isolation or disconnectedness. Often, it's just plain loneliness. It all seems particularly ironic in the contemporary world where we've never been more connected by technology, and yet many people—even those society deems quite successful—find themselves feeling very isolated, alone in the crowd. What's missing for many is a sense of intimacy with other people and the time to savor deep relationships.

Such findings seem to confirm Viktor Frankl's observation that the "truth is that as the struggle for survival has subsided, the question has emerged, 'survival for what?' Today, ever more people have the means to live but not meaning to live for."

In its more pronounced forms, isolation can be a serious, even life-threatening condition, heightening the risks of depression and heart disease. Powerful feelings of isolation can emerge at any age or stage of life, but in the second half of life, when we no longer have the built-in inducements of job or school to impel us to mix with others, the risk tends to be greater. Without a job to go to, many people lose a sense of saving the world; friends die, family members move away, and their sense of savoring it is compromised, too.

In the best-selling *Tuesdays with Morrie,* author Mitch Albom provides a powerful alternative model: his former college professor, Morrie, who, even in his dying days, lives richly through his connections with friends and family and the lessons he passes on to them. And the essence of Morrie's message: "Once you learn how to die, you learn how to live." In authentically sharing this message with his former student, Morrie embodies the spirit of saving and savoring the world: His joyfulness, even in the face of death, arises out of his willingness and ability to really give of himself to help another. In doing so, Morrie more clearly identifies his own "something" to live for, his own special gift to give back to life.

Each of us has a special gift or contribution to which we alone give life—that unique trait or characteristic our loved ones will miss most deeply when we're gone. It's that thing about us that most naturally defines us, the gift we naturally and wholeheartedly give away in all we do—our legacy. For one of us, this may be a sense of humor or perspective; for another, an innate ability to draw people out, to listen. It might be a talent for visualization, or for putting things into words. Or perhaps we naturally are drawn to creating beautiful environments;

or maybe we're the person who others rely on for direction. Whatever it may be, we all have such a gift and long-term happiness in life requires that we express it.

Consequently, one identifying test for this gift is that when we fail to share it, we feel unfulfilled and ultimately disappointed with our lives. Conversely, utilizing this gift in support of a cause we believe in represents the essence of savoring the world by saving it.

Richard's friend and mentor Rollie Larson is a model of someone who has learned this essential truth; Rollie is Richard's "Morrie." And the life lesson he has shared, the gift Rollie naturally gives away is "Listen to someone today!" Listening has been the core practice of his life; he even had bumper stickers made with his signature slogan.

Rollie reflects on attending a WWII veterans' reunion. "Most of my colleagues are dead or too ill to attend. But of those who did make it, many are living in the past, surviving on memories. Many seemed limited in their engagement with life. They're inactive; they sit around watching lots of television. It's self-absorbed living, not much meaning there. I realized, at age 86, I've retooled how I spend my time. I've become more selective in friendships. One of the turnoffs for me is people who don't listen. It's all about them. I call it 'hit-and-run' listening. They're not the kind I spend time with anymore. Talking is a disease—it's like a handicap. Listening is healing for me and for others. Listening is my daily purpose practice."

Complaining About Complaining

The aged curmudgeon—Walter Matthau or Jack Lemmon in *Grumpy Old Men* character—is a staple of popular culture. And it's probably not such a bad thing to develop a cantankerous nature as we age; there are any number of things worth getting worked up over in our later years, from the societal treatment of the elderly to, as Dave's dad used to point out, traffic jams caused by repairs to roads, bridges, and other structures that we won't still be alive to appreciate.

But on the other end of the spectrum, nobody cares for the bitter old man or woman—none the least, that person him or herself.

If you've ever been stuck next to an old sourpuss who just keeps going on and on about how the world has done them wrong, spewing venom and regrets about the way things should be and what could have been (or if you've been that person yourself), you know how tedious that quickly becomes. Moreover, there's something terribly tragic about being the sort of person who has nothing but anger and bile for the way things have turned out in their life and the world.

So we might want to wonder how we can temper our dissatisfactions in the second half of life so that our anger, if we have it, doesn't become all-consuming, so that we hold on to the proper perspective about perceived slights and injustices in the world, so that—while we may on occasion be that curmudgeonly old man or woman—we're not pushing people out of our lives with our anger and not cutting ourselves off from meaningful connections and experiences.

Viktor Frankl's experiences and suffering in WWII served as a human laboratory as Frankl himself writes, ". . . one big experiment—a crucial experiment . . . that proved to us that even under the most deprived, the most humiliating conditions, man can still remain man. . . . It should prove to us what man is and what he can become."

Frankl did not reflect publicly on his own aging until his last book, *Viktor Frankl Recollections: An Autobiography,* in which he wrote, "I don't mind getting old. As I say, aging doesn't bother me as long as I have reason to believe that I am maturing."

If we look at people like Frankl, who have retained a sense of joy and vitality to a very old age, we realize that one of the main tools at their disposal is a capacity to savor the temporal nature of most things. That is, nearly all of the triggers to anger in our lives will—at some not-to-distant point—pass on. Putting them in the perspective of the overall sweep of our lives, we see that all these things that make our blood boil—from someone cutting us off in traffic, to an insensitive word uttered here or there, to a perceived slight from a family member or friend, are mere blips on the radar screen of our existence. Most of what makes us mad, and most of the anger we hold on to is hardly worth the time or energy we apply to it. This isn't to say that there aren't people or events over which we should be righteously angry, but lots of what we get worked up over and stay worked up over doesn't really warrant such attention.

The advice columns in the newspaper are filled with letters from people who have held grudges or have had grudges held against them for years, even decades. And most of what precipitated these feelings strike us as petty: an indiscreet word uttered, a failure to send a thank-you note, a loan not fully repaid, hardly something worth cutting a friend or family member from one's life. Routinely, the advice columnist counsels the person to simply swallow his or her pride and make amends—reasonable advice to be sure, but somewhat pathetic in cases where years and years of possible connections have been lost.

The lesson here is that striving to find meaning is a primary motivational force throughout life. A person's vitality at any stage depends on his or her supply of meaningful connections with self and others. Thus, it's clear that the "crisis" of aging is primarily a crisis of meaning.

This lesson is simple, but profound: We all can do well to examine our lives to complete the connections with others that we have allowed to fray for no particularly good reason. There are few greater losses than the friendship or family connection forsaken simply through stubbornness or inaction. And it's a crying shame to wait until we're on our deathbeds to make those amends. A letter or phone call may be all it takes. And as time in our lives runs out, why waste any more of it?

And, of course, things become more urgent because as we age, some of our capacities inevitably diminish. Most of us, at age 80, won't be able to perform the same feats of athleticism—even if that's only jogging to the refrigerator—that we did at age 30. Our bodies will eventually wear down and we'll find ourselves unable do to things that were easy to us just a few (or so it seems) years ago.

One thing that won't change nearly as dramatically, however, is our capacity for mental activity, at least in the area of creativity. Sure, we may get a bit more forgetful and our attention to detail is apt to waiver, but unless we suffer actual brain damage—a stroke or Alzheimer's for instance—we can continue being as novel in our thinking as ever. We don't have to succumb to the common picture of the doddering old person, stuck in his or her ways.

One simple way to avoid that picture is to practice having one creative thought a day. It doesn't have to be something particularly profound or insightful, it can merely be a new way of looking at something or a fresh idea about how you might do something.

So, for instance, we might practice, on a regular basis, examining our political views or our attitudes about some aspect of society, to see if we still think about things the way we always have. Or we might read a book by an author whose view is one we're unfamiliar with or that we disagree with, simply as an exercise in looking at things differently. Or we could even do something like cook an old familiar recipe but in a different way, with some new ingredients, just so we're not doing everything the way we always have.

The goal is just to have at least one creative thought—something we haven't thought before—every day. And it doesn't even have to be a belief that we end up holding on to; as long as it's novel, that's enough.

The principle is one of creativity and curiosity. We all know the good feeling that ensues from cleaning out an overstuffed closet or bookshelf of items we never wear or refer to anymore. It's the same idea with our mind: It's satisfying to periodically examine what's in our head to see if it's still worth carrying around. And of course, we don't necessarily have to decide about everything all at once. It's always an option to set a thought or attitude back just as we found it for further review at some later date. Or not.

The thing is, if we do this, we're still going to get old and stiff, but at least our thoughts and minds won't be entirely archaic and atrophied. And if we translate this into action, as many thoughtful and committed people do, our chances of living fully only increase.

Holy Discontent

Richard has had the privilege of consulting for Habitat for Humanity International over the past several years and has been inspired over and over by the passion and purpose of the people who work there and those who volunteer with the organization. The so-called "theology of the hammer" is a powerful force for positive change in the world and it emerges directly out of the willingness on the part of those associated with Habitat to put their whole selves into, quite literally, saving the world.

In an inspiring speech at Columbia University on World Habitat Day, Habitat CEO Jonathan Reckford estimated that one in three urban dwellers today is living in poverty; almost a billion people are living in the slums of the largest cities on the planet. Reckford implored his audience, "How do we respond to these statistics? Sometimes people hear such terrible statistics on television and say, 'someone ought to do something about that,' and then they change the channel and watch a movie. That's discontent. But, I think we need 'holy discontent.' That's when we see the same thing and say, 'I can't stand that and I'm going to do something about it.' And then you get off the couch and do it."

Jonathan's own "holy discontent" came several years before coming to Habitat on a mission trip to work with the *dalit* or "untouchable" caste in rural India. He recalls, "Half of these children die before the age of 13, and during my work with them God let me know that I needed to respond."

It was that "holy discontent" that drew him to Habitat. And he observes today that the vast majority of Habitat partners and friends have similarly compelling stories to tell about what drew them to the organization and its work in the world. The common feature is a sense of "holy discontent"—each person became so fed up with an apparent injustice that he or she decided to actually do something about it. Former U.S. Presidents, athletes, elementary school students, church congregations, CEOs of corporations large and small, folks from all walks of life—their "holy discontent" based on a fundamental conviction that everyone deserves a decent place to live led them to Habitat.

The mission of Habitat is to eliminate poverty and homelessness the world over and to make decent shelter a matter of conscience and action. The "holy discontent" shared by many—we should not accept the current state of affairs in which so many are left without a roof over their heads—has led to the construction of more than 225,000 houses, sheltering more than 1,000,000 people in more than 3000 communities in some 100 countries around the world, including all 50 states in the United States.

It took 25 years to build the first 100,000 Habitat houses. The next 100,000 will be built in just five years. Every 24 minutes, someone in the world is walking through the doorway of his or her new Habitat home. Through the "holy discontent" of tens of thousands of volunteers, supporters, and sponsors, hundreds of thousands of low-income families have found new hope in the form of affordable housing. Decent people worldwide, inspired by their own "holy discontent" have joined together to successfully tackle a significant social problem—how to provide decent housing for all.

And yet, when you talk to folks who have taken up the "theology of the hammer," they routinely tell you that they get much more out of the experience than those for whom the houses are being built. The joy they feel from contributing to a cause they believe in more than makes up for the hard work and heavy lifting involved in construction. While each person who participates in Habitat's projects can legitimately be said to be taking part in saving the world, virtually to a person, they all perceive it as entirely a matter of savoring it.

From the moment of birth, we are on the pathway of aging; every day we live we are closer to death. As we make specific passage from one stage of life to another, we all grapple with the aging process and look for answers to one of life's most puzzling questions: How, if death is inevitable, can life be meaningful? And nowadays, with an increased understanding of the fragility of the human species, this question moves from a purely individual level to a societal one.

Thanks to Al Gore's film, *An Inconvenient Truth,* countless people are experiencing "holy discontent" over our need to confront the problem of global climate change. Along with this, more people than ever before urgently want to do something to help. Of course, we can all help in small ways—changing to more efficient light bulbs, recycling more conscientiously, driving less—but many people are looking for ways to make a greater impact.

Eric Utne, founder of the critically acclaimed and highly influential periodical, *The Utne Reader,* found himself at age 60, simultaneously going through a series of major transitions including a divorce and the sale of his magazine. But rather than overwhelming him, these changes inspired in him a stronger desire to make a positive difference in the world.

Inspired by the Council of Elders formed by Nelson Mandela, Jimmy Carter, and other global elders, Eric believes that every city, town, and village in America needs its own local Council of Elders. The Utne Institute, building on the success of the *Utne Reader's* "Neighborhood Salon" movement and its "Let's Talk America" initiative, launched a new program entitled "Earth Councils." These councils of elders are teamed with youth who are energized and committed to positive change.

Earth Councils are groups of local citizens united in their desire to heal, steward, and sustain the Earth, locally and globally. Each is positioned to provide local responses to the planetary climate crisis.

Early in the *Utne Reader's* history, it published a cover story, "Salons: How to Revive the Endangered Art of Conversation and Start a

Revolution in Your Living Room." The magazine immediately got over 10,000 responses and eventually set up some 500 salons, with at least 20 people in each, all across North America. Within a year, 20,000 people had joined the Neighborhood Salon Association, meeting in office conference rooms, church basements, bookstores, coffee shops, and each other's houses to talk about how to change the world for the better—and to do so, as well.

Eric recounts, "The salon movement was born. . . . And now, we think the world is ready for the next generation of citizen gatherings; moving 'beyond salons' to Earth Councils. Our focus now will be to encourage, advise, and support participants as they learn how to transform conversation into action. These councils will combine youth and elders in a collaborative mix based on mutual listening, respect, mentoring, and working together shoulder to shoulder."

Initiatives like Eric's may seem daunting to set out upon, but they are made possible by a series of "holy discontents," each one infused with a sense of joy in the doing of it. Saving the world happens when we savor it each step of the way.

Often what stops people in the second half of life from contributing to causes they believe in, causes inspired by "holy discontent," is a feeling that their time has passed, that they no longer have anything of value to offer. Unfortunately, this is something of a self-fulfilling prophecy. When we denigrate our own potential contributions, it follows that others may as well. This can happen on both an individual and a societal level, "holy discontent" or not.

Or we may refrain from taking actions in support of a cause we believe in or may fail to embark on learning something new—simply because we feel we're not good enough or pure enough or are too old or should know how to do this thing already at this point in our life.

Paul Rogat Loeb, in his book, *Soul of a Citizen,* makes this point in a chapter entitled "We Don't Have to Be Saints." He talks about how many people refrain from making small efforts to better the lives of others because they feel those efforts are too insignificant or insufficiently worthwhile. Often, says Loeb, people censor themselves because they fear they aren't pure enough in their own lives to speak out for causes they feel strongly about. Loeb illustrates this with a story about when he was living in Berkeley, California, and he and some fellow environmental activists needed to travel south to Palo Alto to protest the policies of major oil companies. They were conflicted because their only reasonable way to get there was to drive, which seemed to be at odds with the cause they were lobbying for. Ultimately, writes, Loeb, he and the other protesters decided to live with that contradiction, feeling that the good they were doing by raising the issues outweighed the "impurity" of their mode of travel.

The point here is that, often, what matters most is taking that first step. We can get paralyzed by perfection and end up doing nothing when 99.9% of the time, doing something, anything, is preferable.

In the second half of life, especially for people who have had fairly structured careers, that "What difference will it make?" question can loom large. It's not uncommon for people who are accustomed to being successful to end up doing very little and essentially wasting away because they're too proud or scared or confused to do something that could be construed as less than great.

The alternative to this is action, even if it's not exactly the action you would take if everything were perfect. So, for instance, instead of starting up an international nonprofit agency devoted full-time to providing college scholarships to at-risk kids, you might simply volunteer to tutor at a local school. Rather than taking a round-the-world fully self-supported bicycle trek, you might do as Portland, Oregon, retiree Alan Koch did: set out on a mission to ride down every street in your town. In most cases, a small step is better than no step at all.

Although we want to dream big, we don't want our big dreams to get in the way of our small steps. Just because we can't save the entire world doesn't mean we can't help at least one other person.

So instead of characterizing the second half of our lives in terms of all the things we might do but don't, we begin to experience them as the many things we can do in spite of it all. We don't let planning get in the way of doing or allow possibilities to constrain actualities. Instead of sitting in the old armchair on our porch musing about what we could do if only we were younger, stronger, and more financially independent, we're out in the world, doing something, making a difference, even if it's only to one other person or even just ourselves.

In Christopher Buckley's darkly comic novel, *Boomsday*, Cassandra Devine, a 29-year-old Internet celebrity blogger starts a nationwide political movement among her fellow "Whatever Generation" cohort to encourage Baby Boomers to "voluntarily transition" (that is, commit suicide) at age 70 to prevent all those millions of aging post-World War II men and women from bankrupting Social Security, devastating the national health care system, and, in general, paying for their old age and infirmity on the backs of the young and healthy. Buckley plays the story for laughs but there's certainly an element or two of truth to the scenario he paints. Plenty of young people are more than just slightly peeved at the advantages and benefits enjoyed by older folks—and their point is probably well taken.

To the extent we are able, those of us in the second half of life have a moral imperative to share those advantages and benefits with those in the first half.

It's understandable, however, why we may fail to do so. Many of us in the latter half of our lives have been focused so long on making it, on providing for ourselves and our families, that we've tended, by and large, to overlook the contributions we could (and probably should) make to generations following in our very large wake. Fortunately, reaching out across the years is among our most powerful means of finding and securing ongoing fulfillment in our own lives.

This isn't to say it's easy. The prospect of somehow waltzing into a group of people half our age (or younger), is not only daunting, it's unrealistic. Most of us, by the time we're in our fifties or sixties—unless we are teachers or own a skateboard shop—don't have everyday contact with youth, except maybe our own kids. Consequently a distance is formed, which can lead to distrust and miscommunication on both sides. Contemporary society is organized such that we tend to interact socially and professionally with people around the same age as we are, and this becomes much more pronounced in retirement years. However, this stratification is a source of pain and loss in the lives of both the young and the old.

The challenge, therefore—but the opportunity as well—is to figure out how we can make those connections across the years, and in ways that don't make us seem foolish or pathetic. Easier said than done, of course, but done best, in most cases, when the connections are fostered through activities that sustain all parties involved. So, for instance, we will successfully connect across the generations if we're all doing something that we consider either fun or meaningful or both. Grandpa telling the kids how much better things were when he was a boy is unlikely to earn him many young friends. By contrast, when the old guy joins in (or helps organize) a rally or demonstration in support of streams they all fish in or bike lanes they all ride, then chances for real bonding are much higher.

Intergenerational living arrangements, which for most of human history were the norm, are another way such connections can be fostered. Many "empty-nesters" are exploring housing options with their adult children that allow them to participate more closely in the lives of their grandchildren. Dave's mom, for example, after his father died, purchased a duplex with his sister, so she could be more involved in the rearing of his nephews. Other folks we know have eschewed the retirement community to stay connected to the communities they are part of.

It seems obvious in a way, we just have to find opportunities that make it obvious in our own lives and in ways that make sense for our own situations. One way for those of us on the high side of the age wave can do that is to consider how we have drawn upon the lessons of those younger than us in our own lives and express our gratitude for that assistance.

And one way to do that may be another *Letter to Live For.*

Letter to Live For: Across the Age Divide

To All Those Young Enough To View Us As Old:

We're not, really. Old, that is. We're essentially the same people we were at your age; it's just our bodies that have aged.

Of course, all old people say this; when we heard our granddads say that same thing years ago, we didn't buy it at all. They said they felt like kids in their twenties, but they sure didn't look like it; so we'd be skeptical, too, if we were you, about elder people claiming not to be old.

It's understandable why we do it, though: Don't let anyone over 50 tell you that they don't pine, in some way, for youth. There are some wonderful things about being young, and it's hard for anyone to let them go.

But at the same time, many of us wouldn't go back and trade places with you for anything. We may miss certain aspects of youth, but still have no desire whatsoever to be young again. It's taken us all a long time to get here and the prospect of going back is not at all interesting.

What we do want, however, are stronger, more meaningful connections with you, connections that are not just about our allegedly passing on our "wisdom." After all, a good many of us rejected the lessons of our elders, why should the situation be any different today?

Our overriding goal, of course, is to prepare you for our departure. We want to leave you and the world what you need to carry on after we're gone. That's what human beings have been doing for millennia and we're no different.

Being a wise elder is more about questions than answers. So, here are some questions we have for you: "What are your passions?" "What are your values? "What are your gifts?" "What are you living for, today?"

We ask you what we can do, in this later phase of our lives, to make the current and upcoming phases of your lives better. No doubt this will include, in part, asking the eternal questions with you—having courageous conversations together. But that is something that we are willing to commit to, in the name of a better life, not only for the youth of today, but for those you will (at least if you end up like every other old person in history—and you might not) be asking the same questions in the future.

With love above all,

Your ancestor

Try something like this yourself: Write a letter to the future, a time capsule of sorts. What would you like to ask those who follow in your footsteps? What questions might you pose? What answers would you share? When you're done, you might even try sending it to a younger person you know and see what sort of conversation ensues.

chapter 6

putting your whole self in

Many persons have a wrong idea of what
constitutes true happiness. It is not attained
through self gratification, but through fidelity to a
worthy purpose.

Helen Keller

Content, Not Plumage

⊹)‑(⊹ We have been walking across the stubbly grassland along the edge
of the Serengeti for about two hours. Our group of about a dozen, led
by a Dorobo hunter-gatherer named Toroye, has seen an amazing array
of wildlife: herds of gazelle and impala, chattering monkeys who skirt
around the edges of sight, pointing and taunting, nonchalant zebra
munching passively in the distance. But at the moment, we are transfixed
by a much less impressive animal. Toroye has pointed out to us a totally
nondescript brown bird sitting on a fallen log about 20 yards away. It
sings its characteristic song, "Weet-terr, weet-terr," and we realize that
it is the storied honey-guide, the Indicator Bird, that shows the hunter-
gatherers where to find hives and honeycombs, a staple of their diet.

Daudi cautions us to be quiet as we watch and listen to the bird.
"He is singing to us; there will be a honeycomb in that log."

As we crouch down and take out our binoculars for a closer look,
we must admit that we are less than greatly impressed with our avian
friend. Having heard tell of the honey-guide on many occasions, we
rather expected something more spectacular—a proud and colorful
peacock or a soaring falcon, not this unassuming little thing, no more

visually exciting than a common robin we might see on our lawns back home.

Toroye, though, is visibly excited and in a few moments, we will find out why as he approaches the fallen log and, as the honey-guide rises up and settles on a nearby acacia branch to watch, takes out his machete and cuts into the wood where the bird had previously been sitting. Sure enough, there is the thick ball of a bee's nest within, dripping with nectar and larvae, more than enough for all of us to sample.

Daudi reminds us to leave the waxy comb we've chewed on the log for the honey-guide to eat after we've gone. Tradition says we must thank the bird for guiding us to this bounty or he will refrain from doing so in the future.

As we leave our offering for the bird, we tell Daudi how surprised we are to see that this famous somewhat larger-than-life African archetype is so common-looking. It's amazing that it guided us so effectively to the source of our little feast. We expected a bird that was more striking, more beautiful, not the drab little fellow now picking away at dropped honeycombs nearby.

Daudi laughs and says, "Sometimes it's about content, not plumage," and his words, especially for Toroye, who nods vigorously, ring true. The honey-guide doesn't need to impress with his appearance; his beauty is to be found not in how he looks, but what he does. There are lots of beautiful birds out there everywhere, but only one who has this remarkable connection with man and his environment, only one who guides humans, in this unique symbiotic relationship, to something they need and, in return, receives something he needs as well.

Looking around our group of mostly gray-haired older men, we take Daudi's words to heart. Our own plumage, tempered by the years, is rather dull, too. And yet, we feel confident that what we have to offer each other and our communities is of real value. We have experience and the wisdom, or at least the knowledge and perspective that age brings. We have compassion born of many years caring about and for others. And we have the sense of humor and patience that comes from decades of observing people's faults and foibles, especially our own.

In short, like our contemporaries everywhere in later life, we are more about substance than style, content rather than plumage.

And as the honey-guide has shown us, as he has shown hungry hunter-gatherers from time immemorial, sometimes it *is* about content, not plumage.

Indicators for the Ages

One indicator of vital aging is resilience. Systems that are resilient tend to last. This is true in many aspects of existence, from social organizations, to marriages, to processes and procedures that sustain life on many levels.

Of course, this isn't to say that everything that's old is good; change is inevitable. However, the fact that something is resilient over time can be seen, in general, as a point in its favor.

While on our safari, we had the great good fortune of spending several days with the Hadzabe, one of the last remaining hunter-gathering tribes on the planet still living in their traditional manner. Their current lifestyle is essentially as it has been for their people for thousands, if not tens of thousands of years. They live communally, share everything, have no cultural concept of private property, and have managed to sustain themselves from time immemorial, while neighboring tribes, and indeed civilizations all around the globe have come and gone.

Living in kin groups, sustaining themselves through a combination of foraging and hunting, the Hadza (this is the more commonly used conversational version of the tribe's name) have managed to be resilient for centuries when other civilizations, far more "advanced" than they are, have fallen by the wayside. In the Hadza tradition, unlike any of the surrounding peoples, there is no historical record of famine.

The Hadza's success in surviving over the millennia, in an environment that has been, at times, lethal for others, is evidence that they must be doing something right. Their ways of being, maintained through the years, have proven to be effective in the real world; their proof is beyond "the pudding;" it is made manifest by the continuing authenticity of the Hadza people and the ways that have sustained them.

We might wonder, though, if evolution is all about survival of the fittest, the "selfish gene" propagating itself, why do the Hadza people share with each other—and even visitors—so openly? Why is the Hadza culture a totally giving culture with, traditionally, no real notion of private property at all? Why do the Hadza all share openly, risk their lives to save each other, and volunteer to feed each other through their daily hunting and gathering rituals?

Darwin thought the answer was clear: Altruism evolves from the good of the group:

> There can be no doubt that a tribe including many
> members who, from possessing in a high degree the spirit
> of patriotism, fidelity, obedience, courage, and sympathy,
> were always ready to aid one another and to sacrifice
> themselves for the common good would be victorious over
> most other tribes, and this would be natural selection.

The Hadza exemplify this spirit to which Darwin refers and, in so doing, represent an evolutionary mirror for our own contemporary lives. Theirs is a lifestyle abandoned by others some 10,000 years ago with the dawn of agriculture, yet it is a lifestyle deeply embedded in all our DNA and, as such, has much to teach us—or remind us—about how to live. Although the Hadza live in constant struggle for resources with other groups in Tanzania—pastoralists like the Datoga and agriculturalists like the Iraqw—they have continued to live in their time-honored ways: hunting, gathering, collecting honey, digging tubers, and gathering nuts and berries. That they have been successful in doing this for far, far longer than even the pyramids have stood is testament to the sustainability of their approach to living and a powerful argument for drawing upon their lessons in thinking about how to live our own lives.

Proverbs, sayings, and words of wisdom often dignify the scenes we envision of Hadza lifestyle—the Dark Continent, the ancient hunter-gatherer, the traditional elder—but really, it is far richer than the simplistic picture such scenes may depict. The actual challenges that they face and the remarkable solutions they have come up with to meet those challenges are no less sophisticated in their own way than our culture's most complex technology. When we learn from the Hadza, therefore, we are not learning from people less evolved than we are; we are drawing upon the lessons of masters, especially in regard to the question of what it means to put your whole self into life and community.

Those authentic ways have traditionally been, and to this day continue to be, passed down from the elders in the Hadza community. Elders with experience teach by example and the younger members of the tribe learn by doing. Thus, the authentic wisdom of the tribe is carried on through ongoing practice. As those who are learning come to develop their own expertise, this too cascades forward in the ongoing and successful cycle of resilience.

In the West, we should be so lucky. In our culture, the rapid pace of change makes old ways—even valuable, longstanding ways—obsolete practically overnight. Even when crafts and ways of being do remain sustainable, they are often marginalized as old-fashioned or inefficient or simply not sufficiently "with it."

Our cultural bias tends to be that new is always better and since often it is, the bias tends to be reinforced. Young people are usually more adept at the latest technological innovations than their elders and, as a result, youthful knowledge is typically valued over the wisdom of experience. Again, this isn't always a bad thing—opportunities for young people to teach and guide those older than them are to be welcomed—but often, something important is lost when we value so highly the new and devalue the tried-and-true.

Perhaps it's one of those "throwing out the baby with the bath-water" cases: Because, as a society, we tend to so highly value youthful understanding in the area of technology, we end up devaluing elder wisdom in other areas of life, areas in which that wisdom could truly make a difference. It is up to us, therefore, to separate and clarify those arenas in which the wisdom of experience is most valuable and can make the most positive difference to us all.

Not surprisingly, the authentic ways of traditional cultures like the Hadza can offer, like the honey-guide does, some guidance here. For instance, the oral tradition can provide us with a model for how we may be able to reclaim some hidden aspects of the tenuous connection between young and old in our world.

Among traditional peoples, elders are the story keepers. Those who have lived longest and experienced most become the voice of the collective tribal wisdom. Thus, their stories tend to be about the tribe, rather than the individual, even if the tribal experience is embodied in a story about an individual.

The question we may ask ourselves, then, is: Which of our life's stories embody a perspective that goes beyond our individual experience? What stories can each of us tell about ourselves that seem to have larger meaning than simply the content of our own lives?

Paradoxically, though, the stories that are most authentic usually have the most universal appeal. What we need to do, therefore, is mine our lives for the stories that are most revealing of our true characters. When we tell a story that shows others who we really are, then our listeners learn not only about who we are, but even more importantly, who they are.

When we would sit around the campfire in Africa talking with each other about our lives and dreams, we would always come to know ourselves better by hearing what our fellow travelers said about themselves. Our friend Buck Elliot put it best: "By hearing your stories, I came to know my own better."

Among the most authentic stories we tell are those that explore our ideas about our deepest values and beliefs. But no matter what our core philosophy, it's inevitable that, in the second half of life, we will concern ourselves more with spiritual issues. The "invisible game" necessarily compels us and the "big questions" that we may have set aside return, like waves upon the shore. For some, this may call for a revitalization of lifelong religious practices; for others, the spiritual, which philosopher Robert Solomon has beautifully defined as "a thoughtful love for life," may be found in less structured settings, or out in nature.

In any case, this inevitable spiritual pull represents, once more, Rumi's observation of life's stages as we move from being searchers after wisdom to hunters of more invisible game. And what is more invisible, really, than the sacred?

During the second half, the sacred seems to reassert itself in our daily lives. We find the spiritual dimension touching the practical aspect more and more. The loss of one's parents, for instance, becoming an orphan, is a typical wake-up call that forces us to confront our spiritual perspectives in daily life.

As difficult as such losses can be, they do attune us to seeing the sacred all around—by no means an easy task. Spiritual teachings from time immemorial remind us how difficult it is to obtain and maintain a connection to the feeling that all is sacred. Often, it comes to us in unexpected ways, at unexpected times.

❋ It's the second to last night of our stay in Africa, we are camping in Maasailand, taking day hikes through the grasslands, meeting with elders from the Maasai people, spending the afternoon visiting a traditional boma, where tribespeople live in conjuction with their cattle; late afternoon, and our guide, Daudi, finds out that it's Dave's 49th birthday.

"We've got to get them to roast a goat for you," he proclaims and quickly arranges with our Maasai hosts for this to happen.

A roasted goat is the traditional celebratory offering for various special occasions; it is a great honor to have an animal slaughtered and eaten in your name.

Dave is quite touched by the generosity of this gesture, but he's a bit torn; after all, he has been a vegetarian for almost two decades and generally prefers to see animals in the wild rather than on his plate. And yet, he can't help believing that it would be incredibly rude and insensitive to turn down the offer being made, not to mention a once-in-a-lifetime opportunity missed.

"So what I resolved to do," he says, "is to try to participate wholeheartedly and be as present as I could in all aspects of the animal's preparation. I wanted to be as respectful as I could be both to the goat who would feed us and to the Maasai men who killed, butchered, and cooked it for our group.

"It wasn't that easy for me to stand there and watch the poor creature be smothered, although I must say, it was done with no shred of cruelty and I don't believe the animal suffered at all. One of the men simply held the goat's mouth closed and covered its snout with his hand until the creature stopped breathing. It hardly struggled, really, and did not whimper or cry out.

"The butchering was done with great care and extreme skill; first, the animal was skinned and then, the hide, spread out flat, was used as a kind of table for cutting up the carcass into parts. The Maasai do not bleed the animal, as they consider the blood important to the taste of the meat and to its energetic qualities. Almost all the organs were kept; even the intestine was cleaned and cooked in stew.

"Although I did refrain from participating when the still warm liver was passed around to sample, I did not hesitate later that evening when portions of the cooked animal were offered ceremoniously to us all. I found the meat reasonably tasty, but more importantly, I felt as if

I were wholeheartedly putting myself into an opportunity that life was presenting to me. I suppose I could have done what I would usually do when meat is on the menu and turned it down, but in doing so, I think I would have been saying 'no' to a perfectly clear example of the sort of authentic experience that we intuitively seek in life, especially during the second half. And even more importantly, I would have missed out on an experience that connected me, in a very pure way to something much larger, a tradition that embraces the interconnectedness of life and the sacred in all things."

Learning to put ourselves wholeheartedly into daily life is all about wholeness—growing whole, not old. It involves experiencing a wholehearted connection to what before was separate from us. Spiritual connection takes root deeply only when it endures the trials of daily life. It is through the path of deep presence in daily life that the sacred fully emerges—and we come to understand what we are really living for. In accepting the presence dimension that is inherent in simple, everyday actions, we eventually discover how to savor life.

Whenever the sacred becomes present in the second half of life, a commitment to serve emerges. One can call this "generativity," as Erik and Joan Erikson did, or "stewardship" as do Christians, or "seva" as do Buddhists. But whatever its name, service is a path toward the sacred that opens up both a profound spiritual understanding and a deep joy—it is saving and savoring the world in action. Paths toward the sacred lead us toward what was here before us and will remain after us, in short, the whole of creation.

Throughout history, in indigenous cultures, in the world's religions, we find recognition of the process of spiritual renewal in everyday life. Human cultures recognized that the "self" must undergo renewal or rebirth. At every stage of life—birth, puberty, marriage, childbirth, old age, and death—rites of passage acknowledged change and renewal. If such rites were useful in cultures where the average lifespan was 40, they are even more vital today when the average life expectancy is often double that.

How are you putting yourself wholeheartedly into this phase of your life?

It doesn't so much matter *what* you do (although probably not anything will work), as *that* you do. On the occasion of her fiftieth year, for instance, a friend of ours planted 50 trees as a way of marking her connection to mother Earth.

We encourage you to reflect on your own rite of passage into the next phase of life. And even, if possible, make that rite a reality—for example, what we call *The Annual Purpose Checkup.*

The Annual Purpose Checkup

After a certain age, most of us accept the necessity of regular physical checkups. While the poking and prodding we subject ourselves to on annual basis may not be the most delightful way to spend an afternoon, we recognize that the information gained from the experience makes it worthwhile. Likewise, we're generally willing to review our financial situations with some regularity. Again, the information may not always be what we want to hear, but knowing where we stand is preferable to remaining in the dark.

So, if money, medicine, and meaning are essential to a vital second half of life, we might be wise to take guidance from the financial and medical worlds and adopt the practice of a regular checkup of that third dimension—an annual check-in to see if our spirit, our sense of meaning, remains healthy.

Do we still feel a sense of meaning and aliveness? Is the meaning we have defined for ourselves still consistent with our needs and desires? Are there changes we need to make to reinvigorate a sense of meaning in our lives? Even an hour or so of reflection on such questions can produce positive effects and subtle insights. No matter how meaningful our life may seem, there can still be room for growth.

The *Annual Purpose Checkup* can be keyed to your birthday, so it's easy to remember—and something to look forward to, a gift to yourself on this special occasion. Additionally, this may also be a time when friends and family members are around, and presumably, disposed to help should you want some assistance. Moreover, the *Annual Purpose Checkup* can be another way to celebrate one more year of self-discovery and self-acceptance, a benefit of aging beautifully articulated by Anne Lamott in her book, *Plan B:* "Age has given me what I was looking for my entire life. It has given me me."

You can do the *Annual Purpose Checkup* with greater or lesser degrees of formality, depending on your preference. Some people may undertake it as a retreat, devoting a specific space of time set aside just for that purpose. Others may fit it more closely into their day-to-day lives, and some might simply find moments for reflection, while walking the dog, or taking a drive, or just sitting quietly by themselves. In whatever manner you undertake the *Annual Purpose Checkup,* however, you are should try to reflect on questions that help you examine your work, your relationships, and your sense of connection between who you are and what you're doing in the world.

For instance, how many of the following would you be able to answer in the affirmative?

The Annual Purpose Checkup

- O I work at what I love to do.
- O My daily choices are driven by a strong sense of purpose.
- O I am wholehearted and authentic in my actions and words.
- O There is a clear alignment between what I say my priorities are and how I spend my time.
- O I invest time in making a difference to others in the world.
- O I put my whole self into all that I do.
- O I know what I want to be remembered for.

For each of your "yes" answers, what can you do to sustain this sense of meaning in the year ahead? For the others, what changes can you make to find more meaning in the coming months?

And for all the questions, who can you talk with to expand your understanding of and deepen your appreciation for greater meaning and purpose in your life? Doing so may be the most valuable aspect of the *Annual Purpose Checkup*.

Walking Together

⁜ We are physically, but not yet emotionally recovered from the most harrowing night on our safari. During the journey to this campground, nestled against volcanic buttes high on a plateau in the Serengeti, we experienced real adventure, which continued through the night, even as we bedded down in camp.

We had lingered a bit too long at the interpretive center in the Olduvai Gorge, the so-called cradle of mankind in the Great Rift Valley, awestruck by the landscape and by the connections felt to our first humanoid ancestors 2.5 million years ago. We then fell farther behind our tight schedule being fascinated by the strange phenomenon of the "shifting sands," a 50-foot high sand dune on the high grassy plain that rolls across the Earth about 10 meters a year, pushed by the relentless winds that roar across the pancake-flat landscape.

So it was almost dark as we started off again in our Land Rovers, and fully pitch black as we embarked on an hours-long odyssey in driving rain and lightning, several times almost driving into arroyos so deep that in one, a herd of giraffes were only visible from the head up. Our campground lay in the distance and we had to navigate toward it by dead reckoning, hoping against hope that the flickering light we imagined in the distance was our crew's beacon and not lightning-struck bushes caught on fire.

For a while, it looked like we might be sleeping in our vehicles—if we slept at all—and several members of our party made it abundantly clear that this wasn't what they signed on for—African thrills were one thing, life-threatening drives through an epic thunderstorm were another. Somehow, though, through good luck and perseverance, our drivers found their way to our destination, and we piled out into our soggy camp and relative security, hungry, cold, but at least all in one piece.

The storm raged through most of the night, however, and sleep, for most of us, was fitful, at best. So, when morning dawned, foggy, but calm, and we emerged bleary-eyed from our tents, we all looked pretty shaky, nerves fraying if not frayed.

Conversation around breakfast was quite subdued, therefore; no one cracked jokes, and any comments at all tended to be fairly mundane observations about the weather, as each of us reflected on our experience of the last ten hours or so and the fears and longings it has evoked.

In this sort of mood the two of us, Richard and Dave, set out together, essentially silently, on a walk. Neither of us has planned this; it sort of just happened, as we find ourselves alone together on an ancient path leading through the hills that surround our camp.

Words come slowly at first, but then, as the rhythm of our conversation increases with our walking pace, they flow, and things we have each wanted to say (and probably not even known we've wanted to say) come out easily over the course of the next hour or so.

Here is where the themes of wholeheartedness and authenticity we've tried to explore in this book really emerged. Our conversation comes from the heart, unvarnished by ego, but awash in gratitude. Humbled by our experience of nature's power, we feel no compunction whatsoever to impress each other, or even ourselves, but rather, want only to connect as simply and honestly as we can.

It's an unusual experience for both of us, even though we're good friends, colleagues, and co-authors for almost two decades. It feels as if this is the sort of connection that might occur among comrades on a battlefield, or maybe, if we can imagine this, between hunter-gatherers like the Hadza as they stalk wild game. The words we share are limited, but carry some weight. We don't have to say a lot, but what we do seems to speak volumes. There's no holding back to what we can say, no fear, and no pretence. Our walk together is not long—an hour at most—and yet we return from it changed in how we see one another and in our understanding of who we are.

Did it require an experience that makes our lives flash before our eyes to get to that place? Probably not, but it probably helped. You often hear people say, after one of life's little "wake-up calls," that the experience put things in perspective for them. And that's certainly the case for us. But it's odd, isn't it, that it takes going through something unusual to grasp what is probably the most natural and elemental of all human experiences: a simple sense of presence and connection with another person.

This is what it is, we believe, to really put your whole self into life, to be wholehearted and authentic in the moments you share with others. And this, we believe, is perhaps the best way—if not the only way—to find our way in not just the second half of life, but throughout our days, from cradle to grave. And here, we believe, is the key to finding our way in the second half of life: a combination of saving and savoring the world, where we save by savoring and savor by saving. The two become one, simultaneous, alive, and inseparable.

Viktor Frankl writes, "It is a peculiarity of man that he can only live by looking to the future." He observed that prisoners who lost faith in the future usually died in a short period of time.

How do we maintain faith in the future in the second half of life? The answer Frankl would likely give is that we need to stop asking what we expect of life and start asking what life expects of us. Frankl said, "life ultimately means taking the responsibility to find the right answer to its problems and to fulfill the tasks which it constantly sets for each individual." Putting our whole selves into life means taking the responsibility to find the right answers to life's problems—not just our own, but those of society-at-large.

Starting with gratitude, there's probably nothing more important to putting our whole selves into life than letting those who have helped us or meant something to us or simply put a smile on our faces know how much we appreciate what they have done for us in our lives.

Our lives will be immeasurably richer and more fulfilling if we make the simple effort to express our gratitude to those for whom we are grateful—in person, in a letter, a phone call, even an email can make a difference.

It helps to identify specifically what the person in question has done for you and to be as clear as possible in letting them know how they have made your own life a little better. One way of identifying this is to ask yourself what you would come to that person for by way of help and assistance.

On our Africa trip, Dave tried this exercise with each of the men he had become friends with over the course of the two weeks. Individually, he approached them all and did his best to articulate the unique gift every man had shared—consciously or not—with him. So, for instance, Dave was quite clear that what he would come to Richard for was vision. He expressed his gratitude for the way Richard consistently provided the "big picture" throughout their trip and how he had been long been the visionary force behind their work together.

In a somewhat less solemn example, Dave expressed his gratitude to one of his fellow inventurers, John, who was the best storyteller and jokester on the trip. "I come to you and thank you for all the delight you have given me," is how he put it. And when he shook John's hand warmly, Dave half-expected there to be a joy buzzer in his friend's palm.

Leaving No Trace

Gratitude on a personal level—for those who have helped us on our journey—is mirrored by gratitude for the unseen travelers who follow after us. Consequently, there may be no more wholehearted way to put our whole selves into the second half of life than to lighten our loads—both literally and figuratively.

Many of us have spent our younger days focused on building a life system. We have worked hard and bought many things for ourselves and our families; our houses—and our lives—are filled with all sorts of things, from precious mementos to loads of stuff we can't even recall acquiring.

In a sharing society like the Hadza, this would never be an issue. With no strong sense of private property, individuals simply don't amass a great deal of stuff to be burdened with, or to burden others with. In our world, though it's not uncommon for each of us to have far more things than we can ever keep track of.

There's not anything wrong or unusual about having loads of "stuff"—Dave owns seven bikes, for example; Richard has enough outdoor gear to outfit an expedition to Patagonia. What is crucial, however, is that we make an effort not to clutter the second half of our lives with stuff that weighs us down.

This is true on both the micro and the macro level. It's a given that waste disposal will be among the greatest societal challenges in the twenty-first century and beyond. All our obsolete and unused manufactured goods, all our plastic doo-dads and gimcracks will need to be taken care of; the mountains of discarded cell phones alone are reaching Himalayan proportions.

On an individual level, though, our actual physical possessions may be less of an issue than our emotional, spiritual, and relationship "stuff." It's easy enough, after all, for our survivors to hold an estate sale to dispose of the bikes and tents we've left behind. It's a lot more complicated for our children, friends, and colleagues to get rid of our unresolved issues, unspoken endearments, and unrealized dreams.

So it behooves us to make the ongoing effort in the second half of our lives to lighten our loads: to wholeheartedly deal with the personal and professional situations we've left hanging, to speak the words we've too long held inside, to reach for the goals and experiences we've set aside for one reason or another, to put our whole selves into living simply.

The daily practice for doing this is pretty straightforward. Just as clearing out a physical space is just a matter of doing a little bit at a time—one box a day, for instance—so the task of clearing out emotional space is incremental, as well. A kind word spoken, a letter sent, a visit to a single spot, just one step at a time, and great progress can be made.

Typically, the prospect of dying penniless is considered a tragedy, but seen in another light, we might view it as something to aspire to. After all, if we've used up and/or given away everything by the time we have, as Shakespeare put it, "shuffled off this mortal coil," then we've no doubt done both a pretty good job of both accomplishing all we'd set out to do, but even more, making sure that those who follow in our wake aren't having to take care of business that we could or should have ourselves.

We might construe this as adopting the "leave no trace" philosophy of adventuring as applied to our "inventure" lives. While indeed, we all want to leave a legacy that carries on after we're gone, we do well to live in a way that doesn't destroy the experience for those coming along afterward.

And the choice in this matter is open to all of us. It's simply a matter of doing a little daily practice, as our days in the second half of our lives unfold.

That's What It's All About

➳꙰꙳ The small dark-skinned man bends over the smoking tuft of dried grass and blows gently to ignite it. Spinning a wooden fire stick while applying downward pressure on a fireboard ignites a small coal of tinder. Over the newly ignited flame, he passes his slender arrow, warming it, softening the wood ever so slightly. He takes the shaft of the arrow between his teeth and clenches down, working out the almost imperceptible bends in it. He takes the arrow from his mouth, sights it for straightness, repeating the process with this and several other arrows until he is ready to move out.

His name is Alito and he speaks in the ancient "click" language, inviting his comrades, including several of our group, to join him. On his feet are sections of motorcycle tires shaped into sandals. These are recent additions to the Hadza hunter-gatherer way of life; little else has changed for the lifestyle of these people in the last 30,000 years.

For us, however, it is all new.

It has been, and continues to be a remarkable day for us all. We are walking with the last of the hunter-gatherers on this planet, only 50 kilometers from the Olduvai Gorge, in northern Tanzania, where Louis and Mary Leakey made their breakthrough discoveries of hominid evolution dating back 3.6 million years. The footprints of the hunter-gatherer ancestors, before our eyes, lead back in a direct line to the very origins of humanity. This is the path we are following on our own hunt for the invisible game.

Although they have made this land their home for centuries, it is not easy to find the Hadzabe. Long hours of Land Rover bumping and grinding along dusty and muddy roads strewn with jagged rocks and fallen branches, followed by a tortuous hike through tall grass under a relentless sun have at last yielded this rare contact. About 1000 Hadza live in this region, but they are spread out in mobile bush camps, and not easy to locate.

We're traveling with Dorobo Safaris, a wilderness-oriented walking safari company well known for their values of sustainability and local control and deeply respected among the Hadza. Two young Hadza men emerge from the bush and greet us warmly, "Mutana" (hello) and "It-ik-wa-ta?" (How are you?)

"Bocho bocho!" (Come!) they reply and help us locate their fellow tribe members at the bush camp nearby.

We come upon a scene that while unique in almost all our

experiences, seems strangely familiar, programmed, as it most surely
is, into the deepest part of our collective unconsciousness: On a large
grassy knoll dotted with small acacia trees and several grass huts, ranged
about are several dozen men, women, and children, alone or in small
groups, engaged in various domestic tasks, including arrow-making, tool-
sharpening, and fire-tending. Several of the little ones play a game like
jacks with small round rocks.

Alito is a small man with a wide smile and bright sparkling eyes. He
laughs easily and often, the look on his face tells you he is deeply contented
with his life. His wife, a woman even smaller than he, emerges from their
grass shelter, greeting our safari leader Daudi generously, but shyly. She
carries a baby on her back and a digging stick in her hands, an important
tool for unearthing the hidden tubers that are a staple of the Hadza diet.

We are invited by Alito and his wife to join among his people, and
our group slowly fans out among the village; each of us is made to feel
at home quite quickly. The mood of the camp is extremely comfortable;
no one seems in a hurry to get anywhere or do anything; the time is now,
and whatever each person—young, old, or in-between—is doing is fine.

After a while, though, the level of chatter among the Hadza increases
until suddenly, cued by indicators that most of us visitors fail to see, they all,
almost in unison, rise and begin heading off away from the camp together.
There is among them, an almost celebratory mood; it feels to us like kids
heading out from the classroom onto the playground for recess.

Fifteen to twenty minutes of walking and the group settles down
onto a hillside beneath some shade-giving trees. The women in the group
produce sharpened sticks and begin digging for underground tubers.
Soon, there is a large pile of the yam-like vegetable roasting on a fire.
They are shared all around, even with those of us who only observed the
digging and cooking.

After eating, we spend another hour or so casually sharing stories
and comparing gear. The young Hadza are fascinated with our binoculars;
most of us are equally taken with their bows and honey-axes.

In the evening, back at our camp, we are rejoined by a group of about ten Hadza men, our guides from the afternoon, and several others, elders, one in particular whom we are all amazed by. A spry and leathery little elf of a man, his name is Kampala, and he is the oldest, and arguably the wisest of the Hadza, pegged by his peers at somewhere between 94 and 98 years of age. He has outlived the average life expectancy of his people by at least a factor of two. Yet his age doesn't seem that special to him, although he does admit to being surprised at times he is "still here."

We are offered a demonstration of how the Hadza harvest honey from a beehive in a baobab tree and when the youngster doing the harvesting, Mwapo, throws the honeycomb down from the upper branches to the ground, Kampala is across the grass in a split second to claim his first share. Unabashed in his appetite and desires, Kampala has us all in stitches at his sheer vitality and aliveness.

Later, after nightfall, we receive a vivid illustration of his role among his people and the degree to which his wisdom permeates their shared experience. Kampala, through our guide and translator, Daudi, shares with us a long and rambling, but endlessly compelling version of the Hadza creation story, a dramatic and complex tale of a young girl, her warrior suitor, and her man-eating giant of a father. The younger Hadza men listening to him have the same rapt look of attention on their faces that we have seen in our own children as they watch a Spielberg movie— that's how powerful Kampala is in the oral tradition. The details he shares are rich, but in many ways, secondary.

At one point, one of the other elders, Phillipo, a man of about 70 or so, interrupts to correct Kampala on a point of fact regarding one of the animals in the story, the black mamba snake. "The black mamba's tongue is not purple, it's blue," he says. Kampala shoots back, "Blue, purple, what's the difference? I'm telling a story here and purple works for the story!" The Hadza, young and old, erupt in laughter, and once the interaction is translated for us, we do, too.

After completing his culture's creation story, Kampala asks that we share ours. Our group, which fortunately includes a physicist, cobbles together a version of the Big Bang and Darwinian evolutionary theory. We make the point that in our creation story, the tribes of the Olduvai Gorge, including the Hadza, are the first people. We all come from the Hadza, and, therefore, in a very real way, are all, at our essence, Hadza, too.

At this, there is a flurry of conversation among Kampala and his fellow hunter-gatherers. We ask Daudi what is being discussed and eventually it comes out. It turns out that the Hadza are talking about a different creation story they have than the one Kampala shared with us. It is one only internal to their people, rarely if ever shared with outsiders. And it begins, Daudi tells us, "In the beginning, the Hadza were baboons. . ." We are humbled to be made privy to this unique evolutionary story that the Hadza are aware of. This genuine moment of cross-cultural connection floors us all, Westerner and African alike, and leads, in a while, to the Hadza men sharing with us a number of their traditional songs, hauntingly beautiful call-and-response melodies, similar in some ways to Southern spirituals we have heard, a few with dance accompaniment that Kampala leads.

Afterward, Kampala asks our group to sing a few of our own traditional songs. We offer up "If I Had a Hammer," and "This Little Light of Mine." When he asks for one with a dance, we scratch our heads a bit, but then eventually settle on the only such tune we all know, the "Hokey-Pokey." Tentatively, but with increasing verve, we begin, "You put your left leg in, you take your left leg out, you put your left leg in and you shake it all about. You do the hokey-pokey and you turn yourself around, that's what it's all about."

And this, then you have to picture: Some 20 or so men around a campfire in Africa, Americans, Europeans, and Hadza alike, all dancing together doing the hokey-pokey. Kampala rises and joins us, and when we get to the final verse, "You put your whole self in," leaps in and out with the rest of us, crying "Nzuri sana!" (Very fine!)

And it seems in this moment that it is all there: the authenticity and wholeheartedness, exactly what we have all come to Africa to experience, however fleetingly.

You put your whole self in, that's what it's all about.

The challenge, of course, is how to keep this feeling extant and how to integrate it fully into our lives and work in the "real world."

How do we continue to put our "whole self in" to whatever we do? That's the question that remains with us and that we find ourselves asking over and over.

How can we put our whole self into the second half of our lives?

We can mine the experience of the first half of our lives to enjoy unsurpassed richness in the second half. All it takes is to maintain that connection between where we are in life and where we've come from, drawing upon what we've learned to serve others in some way.

Throughout this book, we have talked about the value of writing letters as a practice whose value cannot be underestimated. Not only do we gain insight into ourselves by doing so, but being able to look back upon our lives recorded in words provides another mirror in which we can see ourselves more clearly.

Developing an ability to share stories from our lives is another means by which we both make meaning in our own lives and pass that on to others. And, as Kampala reminds us, getting all the details just right is not as important as getting the gist of the story and its message on the mark. Names and dates don't matter nearly as much as themes and lessons.

What is key, though, is reflection and self-discovery. We must, after all, find our own self and communicate with it if we are to make meaningful connections and communicate with feeling to others.

♞ *Letter to Live For: To Your Younger Self*

Here is a *Letter to Live For* that can help us clarify those connections between our past and our future. Imagine that you really could "know then what you know now." What lessons that you've learned later in life might have served you along the way? Take this opportunity to write a letter to yourself at a younger age, when advice from your older self, even if it wouldn't have been taken, might have helped.

Here's Dave's sample to himself at age 17, in 11th grade.

Dear Dave,

If I know you—and I assure you, I do—this letter from your future self will fall upon deaf ears. You've never been one to take a lot of advice from others, and at 17, that character trait was probably at its apex.

So, I'm not going to fill this little note with suggestions about how you should or shouldn't live your life—I know you'd probably ignore them anyway.

Instead, I'm going to reflect on how I recall you (that is, me) as an 11th grader and remind you of some of what you've got going for you that you may not always be aware of.

So first, I want to commend you on your enthusiastic embrace of life, Dave. You are a pioneer of new experiences and your willingness to dive right into things you haven't tried before is one of the qualities that will serve you best throughout your days. Don't lose it!

Second, sort of on the flip side, I want to thank you for a kind of basic level-headedness that has seen you, sometimes surprisingly, survive relatively intact through some fairly turbulent times. You've done and will do some stupid things, but I'm glad you've got a kind of "governor" on some of the most potentially dangerous possibilities. Thanks for your survival instinct and for making it alive through your teens and twenties.

Don't ever stop being motivated, as you are now, by love. Face it; you're a romantic. You're going to make a number of mistakes along the way and do a bunch of things you'd be well-advised not to, but by and large, the reason you did them—because you cared deeply for someone or something—was sound. I want to remind you therefore, that any choice motivated by love—even if it doesn't turn out as hoped—is probably the right one.

And then finally, I do want to slip in a tiny bit of advice, but I think it's advice you might take, because you're already pretty much doing it anyway: Don't be afraid to try things just because you're no good at them or because you might fail. The only real regrets you will carry in your life are over the things you haven't done, not those you have. So, if an opportunity to learn something or go somewhere or put yourself on the line over something you believe in presents itself, go for it. You won't regret having tried and not succeeded; you'll only regret having not tried at all.

Oh, and one last thing related to that: you know that girl you're taking to the concert at the end of the school year? Well, she likes you and you should kiss her when the opportunity presents itself; don't miss out!

Have fun,

Dave

passing the axe

Consider what you want to do later in life while you are still young. If you associate enough with older people who enjoy their lives, who are not stored away in any golden ghettos, you will gain a sense of continuity and of the possibilities for a full life.

Margaret Mead

⁺⃛𝇍⁺ As we walk with the Hadza, we are imbued with a sense of aliveness, a feeling of connection to the Earth, to each other, and to ourselves. This mood is probably most exemplified by a young boy, 8 to 10 years old at most, who, with his honey-axe in hand, is leading a group of about half a dozen older boys and men as they make their way down the sloping grassland among the acacia trees. There is much talking and laughing among them; it is clear that they are good-naturedly giving the kid a hard time about his skill in finding and retrieving honey from the surrounding area.

Suddenly, the boy stops and points to the branch of an acacia tree above us. He has seen what no one else has: a tiny cylinder, no bigger than the tip of a drinking straw, poking out from a knot in the tree from which the branch extends. This, we learn, is the passageway that the local stingless bees in season use to enter and exit from their nests hidden in the hollow crooks of tree branches.

In a flash, the boy has scurried up the tree and is hacking away at the knot with his machete. Around the base of the tree, the group of his elders has gathered. They joke with each other and kibbitz the boy as he chips away at the tree, his eyes intent and his face screwed up in concentration.

In just a few moments, the boy has chopped the branch off the tree and brought it to the ground. His group of watchers circles closer around him as he now focuses the effort of his machete on the knot in which he believes the hive is hidden.

At first it seems as though the boy has indeed made a mistake. Chopping more deeply into the tree's knot, he fails, at first, to reveal a nest. And here, the tone of the good-natured ribbing from his assembled tribe members changes ever so slightly. Now, even they continue to tease him, there is more of an air of pulling for him to succeed. The mood has changed from one of resistance to one of care; it's like the underlying support that has been there all along is being allowed to surface. A bit of a hush falls over the assembled; they seem to be holding their collective breath as the boy continues chopping into the wood.

Suddenly, a great smile breaks over the kid's face and a burst of laughter erupts from his watchers. The boy thrusts his thumb and forefinger into the wood and pulls it back, dripping with honey. The group encircles him, patting him on the back and sidling up to partake of the nectar themselves. The boy passes out chunks of the honeycomb while other tribe members help themselves.

It is a moment of small triumph for the kid; he has, in this moment, become a real provider for his people. He has made an authentic contribution to the ongoing sustenance of his people and has been recognized in his people's own way, for doing so.

The Sweetness of Ripening

Those of us who have known elders whose second-half lives have been exemplars of something to live for are fortunate indeed, for from them, we will have seen the special gifts that can come with age. We are blessed to know men and women who, when they reach the age of 60 or 70, begin to free themselves from the constraints of life's first half and begin to express themselves in ways they had not dared to before. Such elders are no longer defined by what others think of them; they are people who define themselves in and on their own terms. Increasingly freed from the burden of having always to adapt to fulfill others' expectations, they graciously pass the axe on to the next generation. Still committed to both saving and savoring the world, they begin to take on new roles in their multigenerational worlds.

Instead of thinking of the second half of life as a descent, they accept the limitations that arise as their bodies slow down and see the transitions they are going through as a new, yet different kind of ascent—a fresh opportunity to ground themselves in a deeper sense of a greater wisdom. Their gratitude for others and for the world becomes more pronounced. They increasingly lighten their loads by letting go of the minutiae and nonessentials of life. Their perspective shifts as a larger picture of life comes into focus. They are able to embrace living with a joy unavailable to them at an earlier age, before understanding had fully blossomed.

Maybe you, too, know someone like this. Maybe you are or are becoming someone like this. These are people who do not conform to our culture's current expectations of retirement and aging. No longer driven by the tasks that shaped the first half of their lives, these new elders' lives become more about meaning than achievement, more about community than competition, more about being than doing. They experience the second half of life as a time of deepening generosity and expansion of the soul—what Wendell Berry calls "the sweetness of ripening."

That said, there is no doubt we are all products of a society that teaches us that aging is descent. We are taught that maturity signals the end of meaningfulness and that to grow old is to grow irrelevant. And yet, experience tells us that these assumptions are false. Vitality is not the exclusive domain of youth, nor is relevancy.

⌒

Often, in our fifties—and certainly in our sixties—we come to grips with the fact that we are moving through middle life, but we don't yet feel "old." Something deep within us is shifting and it's difficult to name or understand. We may feel alone in undergoing this uneasiness or that there is something wrong with us. We develop a clearer sense that one phase of life is ending, but we're not sure what will replace it.

An ancient Hadza saying goes something like, "The eyes of the Hadza never get lost once they have seen something." Literally, it is a testament to their unsurpassed skills as trackers, but in another sense it refers to their collective social memory, their recollections over the millennia, passed down from one generation to another. These stories and folkways have sustained the Hadza people from time immemorial, the deep cultural and spiritual foundation upon which their continued survival has depended. Visiting with them, we witnessed this oral tradition in action, saw how information was transferred through words and behaviors, and were amazed by the liveliness and energy of this transference in all its forms.

The second half of life is ideally about "never getting lost once we have seen something."

So what will it take to find our way in the second half of life? How can we "never get lost" now that we have seen life's first half?

For some time in his professional coaching practice, Richard has used a model called "the Life Spiral," which asks people to project their years left to live based on age, health, and parents' longevity. The shift, from counting up the years we have lived to counting down the years we have left represents a profound shift in perspective for many of us and compels us to find our way, with a new sense of something to live for.

Without something to live for, we die. With something to live for, we experience the second half of our lives with meaning and purpose. Purpose is the one thing that cannot be taken from us. Our purpose is, ultimately, the something we live for. It is the quality or thread we choose to shape our lives around, at all of life's stages.

There comes a time in all our lives, though, when time is of the essence, when our "life spiral" is spiraling out and we no longer have forever to live. We must put our whole selves into life, now. Admitting that is the first step, and quite a first step it is.

But our path forward can be seen more clearly. Spend time with the elders of your own "tribe." Befriend and learn from them. Invite them to tell you the stories of their lives. Find these older mentors who will lead you toward wisdom.

One of the things we love about the people we have known who have exemplified the most vital kind of aging is that they have found strength and joy in self-acceptance. They know and respect who they are and they have discovered a means of engaging with the world that allows them to express themselves and that gives them joy.

We invite you, then, to sit quietly for a moment and envision yourself as such an elder—imagine yourself at, say, age 100.

Recall the gifts you love, that you came to life to share, the ones, that as Richard Bolles suggests, you have agreed before you were born to give in service to your mission here on Earth. Picture how others have benefited from these gifts. What is the legacy you are passing on?

Now, take a first step. Look into a mirror and observe the "sweetness of ripening" in your own face. Appreciate the sense of meaning and purpose in your gaze. Stay as long as it takes to see beyond the outer image, to fully appreciate yourself just the way you are.

What is this person in the mirror's "something to live for?"

And as you see it in your eyes, feel that sense of something to live for burning brightly within, as you find your way by wholeheartedly and authentically putting your whole self into the second half of life.

notes

Chapter 1

20 "Old men ought to be explorers," T. S. Eliot, "East Coker" (1940) in *Four Quartets.*

20 "If the world were merely seductive," E. B. White. Quoted in "E. B. White: Notes and Comment by Author," Israel Shenker, *New York Times,* July 11, 1969.

21 *About Schmidt* (New Line Cinema Productions, 2002).

Chapter 2

28 Derek Walcott, "Love After Love," *Collected Poems 1948–1984* (Farrar, Straus and Giroux, 1986).

32 "All my life I've been taught how to die," Billy Graham, "Pilgrim's Progress," *Newsweek,* August 14, 2006.

32 "One should not search," Viktor E. Frankl, *Man's Search for Meaning: An Introduction to Logotherapy* (Beacon Press, 1962).

34 Frederick Buechner, *Wishful Thinking: A Seeker's ABC* (HarperOne, 1993).

34 Eugene O'Kelly, *Chasing Daylight: How My Forthcoming Death Transformed My Life* (McGraw-Hill, 2005).

38   "The fear of death is the basic fear," Ernest Becker, *The Denial of Death* (Free Press, 1998).

38   "The confronting of death," Rollo May, *The Discovery of Being: Writings in Existential Psychology* (W. W. Norton, 1994).

39   Stephen Levine, *A Year to Live: How to Live This Year As If It Were Your Last* (Harmony/Bell Tower, 1998).

40   Erik Erikson, *Childhood and Society* (Hogarth Press, 1964).

Chapter 3

56   "Age is no better," Henry David Thoreau, *Walden* (1854).

58   Robert Coles, *The Spiritual Life of Children* (Houghton Mifflin, 1990).

62   *Groundhog Day* (Columbia Pictures Corporation, 1993).

67   *The Ultimate Gift* (Dean River Productions, 2006).

68   Dan Wakefield, *The Story of Your Life: Writing a Spiritual Autobiography* (Beacon Press, 1990).

68   Mary Oliver, "The Summer Day," from *New and Selected Poems, Volume One* (Beacon Press, 1992).

68   "You can and should write an ethical will," Andrew Weil, *Healthy Aging: A Lifelong Guide to Your Physical and Spiritual Well-Being* (Knopf, 2005).

71   Rachel Freed, *Heartmates: A Guide for the Spouse and Family of the Heart Patient* (Fairview Press, 2002) and *Women's Lives, Women's Legacies: Passing Your Beliefs and Blessings to Future Generations* (Fairview Press, 2003).

72   "Why were you not Moses?" Martin Buber, *Between Man and Man* (first published 1947).

Chapter 4

82   Robert Butler, *Why Survive? Being Old in America* (Harper & Row, 1975).

83   "What we seek constantly," Robert A. Johnson, *We: Understanding the Psychology of Romantic Love* (HarperCollins, 1983).

85   *Emmanuel's Gift* (Lookalike Productions, 2005).

89   Richard Nelson Bolles, *What Color Is Your Parachute? A Practical Manual for Job-Hunters and Career-Changers* (Ten Speed Press, updated annually).

89   "One should not search," Viktor E. Frankl, *Man's Search for Meaning: An Introduction to Logotherapy* (Beacon Press, 1962).

96   Betty Friedan, *The Fountain of Age* (Simon & Schuster, 1993).

96   Rabbi Zalman Schachter-Shalomi, *From Age-ing to Sage-ing: A Profound New Vision of Growing Older* (Warner Books, 1997).

Chapter 5

105   Thomas J. Stanley and William D. Danko, *The Millionaire Next Door: The Surprising Secrets of America's Wealthy* (Longstreet Press, 1996).

106   Mitch Albom, *Tuesdays with Morrie: An Old Man, a Young Man, and Life's Greatest Lesson* (Doubleday, 1997).

108   Viktor Frankl, *Viktor Frankl Recollections: An Autobiography*, translated by Joseph and Judith Fabry (Plenum Press, 1997).

113   *An Inconvenient Truth* (Lawrence Bender Productions, 2006).

113   "Salons: How to Revive the Endangered Art of Conversation and Start a Revolution in Your Living Room," *Utne Reader*, 1991.

114   Paul Rogat Loeb, *Soul of a Citizen: Living with Conviction in a Cynical Time* (St. Martin's Press, 1999).

116   Christopher Buckley, *Boomsday* (Twelve, 2007).

Chapter 6

124   "There can be no doubt," Charles Darwin, *The Descent of Man* (second edition, 1874).

127   Robert C. Solomon, *Spirituality for the Skeptic: The Thoughtful Love of Life* (Oxford University Press, 2002).

131 Anne Lamott, *Plan B: Further Thoughts on Faith* (Riverhead Books, 2005).

134 Viktor E. Frankl, *Man's Search for Meaning: An Introduction to Logotherapy* (Beacon Press, 1962).

Epilogue

147 "the sweetness of ripening," in "Ripening," Wendell Berry, *The Collected Poems of Wendell Berry, 1957–1982* (North Point Press, 1987).

index

about the authors

Richard J. Leider

Ranked by *Forbes* magazine as one of the *Top 5 Most Respected Executive Coaches*, Richard is a pioneer in the field of coaching. Founder and Chairman of The Inventure Group, a coaching firm in Minneapolis, MN, Richard has a worldwide coaching practice with many leading executives and organizations. As a seminar leader, he has taught over 100,000 executives from 50 corporations. Richard is a popular speaker and a best-selling author and co-author of eight books, including *The Power of Purpose* and *Repacking Your Bags*, both considered classics in the life/work planning field. A Nationally Certified Master Career Counselor, Richard holds a Master's degree in Counseling and is a Senior Fellow at the University of Minnesota's Center for Spirituality and Healing. Along with his professional pursuits, he has been leading Inventure Expedition walking safaris for 25 years in Tanzania, East Africa. Believing that each of us is born with a purpose, Richard's purpose is to help people "discover the power of purpose."

David A. Shapiro

David Shapiro is a philosopher, educator, and writer whose personal and professional interests revolve around questions of meaning and morality in life and work. He is a tenured faculty member in philosophy at Cascadia Community College outside Seattle, WA, and the co-author of three other books with Richard Leider, most recently, *Claiming Your Place at the Fire: Living the Second Half of Your Life on Purpose* (Berrett-Koehler, 2004.) Additionally, David is Education Director of the Northwest Center for Philosophy for Children, a nonprofit that brings philosophy and philosophers into schools and community organizations around the Pacific Northwest. He defines his purpose as "creating community through dialogue and reflection."

finding your way resources

Reading a book can be very helpful to finding your way and we hope that this book has been useful to you in finding yours.

In this book we have shared what we have learned from many experiences, teachers and life stories. We invite you to participate in an on-going conversation as you find your way in the second half of life. If anything in this book touched you, troubled you, or inspired you, please e-mail to tell us. We are interested in hearing about sources, resources, and stories of people finding their way. We'll respond.

e-mail: info@inventuregroup.com

You can carry on the process of finding your way with products and programs offered by Richard Leider, including:

- Keynote Speeches
- Workshops
- Coaching
- Expeditions
- Online Resources

contact: www.RichardLeider.com

The Inventure Group along with the University of Minnesota's *Center for Spirituality and Healing* have collaborated to create The Purpose Project—to open up new conversations and possibilites for people entering the second half of their lives, including:

- Research
- Workshops
- Conferences
- Guild Training

for more information, contact: www.csh.umn.edu

More books from Richard Leider and David Shapiro

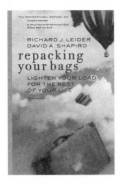

repacking your bags

LIGHTEN YOUR LOAD
FOR THE REST
OF YOUR LIFE
2ND EDITION

Richard J. Leider and David A. Shapiro

Learn how to climb out from under the many burdens
you're carrying and find the fulfillment that's missing
in your life. A simple yet elegant process teaches you to
balance the demands of work, love, and place in order to
create and live your own vision of success.

Paperback, 260 pages
ISBN 9781576751800
Item #51805

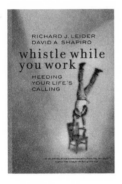

whistle while you work

HEEDING YOUR LIFE'S CALLING

Richard J. Leider and David A. Shapiro

We all have a calling in life. It needs only to be uncovered,
not discovered. *Whistle While You Work* makes the
uncovering process inspiring and fun. Featuring a
unique "Calling Card" exercise—a powerful way to put
the whistle in your work—it is a liberating and practical
guide that will help you find work that is truly satisfying,
profoundly fulfilling, and consistent with your deepest
values.

Paperback, 200 pages
ISBN 9781576751039
Item #51031

the power of purpose
CREATING MEANING IN YOUR LIFE AND WORK
Richard J. Leider

We all possess a unique ability to do the work we were made for. Concise and easy to read, and including numerous stories of people living on purpose, *The Power of Purpose* is a remarkable tool to help you find your calling, and an original guide to discovering the work you love to do.

Paperback, 170 pages
ISBN 9781576753224
Item #53220

claiming your place at the fire
LIVING THE SECOND HALF OF YOUR LIFE ON PURPOSE
Richard J. Leider and David A. Shapiro

Never before have so many entered the second half of life so vital, healthy, and free. And never before have so many had such a hunger for direction in how to live this stage of their lives in a purposeful way. *Claiming Your Place At the Fire* helps us embrace the lessons that we learn as we age and share these lessons in a manner that is relevant and meaningful.

Paperback, 170 pages
ISBN 9781576752975
Item #52976

BK
Berrett–Koehler Publishers, Inc.
San Francisco
a BK Life book

Berrett-Koehler Publishers • PO Box 565, Williston, VT 05495-9900
Call toll-free! 800-929-2929 7 am-9 pm EST Or fax your order to 1-802-864-7626
For fastest service order online: www.bkconnection.com

about berrett-koehler publishers

Berrett-Koehler is an independent publisher dedicated to an ambitious mission: Creating a World That Works for All.

We believe that to truly create a better world, action is needed at all levels—individual, organizational, and societal. At the individual level, our publications help people align their lives with their values and with their aspirations for a better world. At the organizational level, our publications promote progressive leadership and management practices, socially responsible approaches to business, and humane and effective organizations. At the societal level, our publications advance social and economic justice, shared prosperity, sustainability, and new solutions to national and global issues.

A major theme of our publications is "Opening Up New Space." They challenge conventional thinking, introduce new ideas, and foster positive change. Their common quest is changing the underlying beliefs, mindsets, and structures that keep generating the same cycles of problems, no matter who our leaders are or what improvement programs we adopt.

We strive to practice what we preach—to operate our publishing company in line with the ideas in our books. At the core of our approach is stewardship, which we define as a deep sense of responsibility to administer the company for the benefit of all of our "stakeholder" groups: authors, customers, employees, investors, service providers, and the communities and environment around us.

We are grateful to the thousands of readers, authors, and other friends of the company who consider themselves to be part of the "BK Community." We hope that you, too, will join us in our mission.

A BK Life Book

This book is part of our BK Life series. BK Life books change people's lives. They help individuals improve their lives in ways that are beneficial for the families, organizations, communities, nations, and world in which they live and work. To find out more, visit www.bk-life.com.

be connected

Visit Our Website

Go to www.bkconnection.com to read exclusive previews and excerpts of new books, find detailed information on all Berrett-Koehler titles and authors, browse subject-area libraries of books, and get special discounts.

Subscribe to Our Free E-Newsletter

Be the first to hear about new publications, special discount offers, exclusive articles, news about bestsellers, and more! Get on the list for our free e-newsletter by going to www.bkconnection.com.

Get Quantity Discounts

Berrett-Koehler books are available at quantity discounts for orders of ten or more copies. Please call us toll-free at (800) 929-2929 or email us at bkp.orders@aidcvt.com.

Host a Reading Group

For tips on how to form and carry on a book reading group in your workplace or community, see our website at www.bkconnection.com.

Join the BK Community

Thousands of readers of our books have become part of the "BK Community" by participating in events featuring our authors, reviewing draft manuscripts of forthcoming books, spreading the word about their favorite books, and supporting our publishing program in other ways. If you would like to join the BK Community, please contact us at bkcommunity@bkpub.com.